Psychometric
Tests for
Graduates

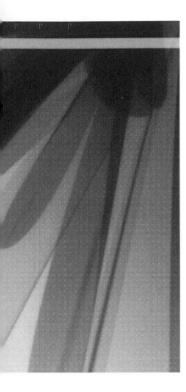

Psychometric Tests for Graduates

Andrea Shavick

howtobooks

Published by How To Books Ltd,
3 Newtec Place, Magdalen Road,
Oxford OX4 1RE. United Kingdom.
Tel: (01865) 793806. Fax: (01865) 248780.
email: info@howtobooks.co.uk
http://www.howtobooks.co.uk

Reprinted 2005

British Library Cataloguing in Publication Data
A catalogue record for this book is available from the British Library

Cover design by Baseline Arts Ltd, Oxford
Produced for How To Books by Deer Park Productions
Typeset by PDQ Typesetting, Newcastle-under-Lyme, Staffs.
Printed and bound by Bell & Bain Ltd, Glasgow

Contents

Acknowledgements

My thanks to the following people for their help and advice: Roy Davis and Tracy Luckett of SHL Group plc, Graham Shavick of Sainsbury's Supermarkets Ltd, Daniel Shavick and Nikki Read at How To Books.

Introduction

So the party's over and now you've got to find a job ... and if you thought university was hard work, you wait!

The good news is there are thousands of brilliant firms out there, offering everything from sky-high salaries, profit-related bonuses, long holidays, flexible working, mentor schemes, staff discounts, free shares, free canteens, health and life insurance, sponsored higher degrees, advanced training, gyms, outings, holidays ... you name it. But first you'll have to get in.

Unfortunately the days when all you needed was a great CV and a sparkling performance at interview are long gone. Now you also need to be able to pass a whole range of psychometric and management tests with flying colours. That's what this book is all about.

In this book I explain all there is to know about psychometric and management tests; what they are, what they measure, who uses them, why they're used, how to survive them, and even how to avoid them altogether! Have a look at the Contents section to see just how much is included.

Also included are **37 different practice tests** for you to try. If you want to improve your test scores dramatically, the best way to do it is to practise.

By the way, the tests in this book are not 'made up' tests that you sometimes see in books about psychometrics, nor are they puzzles or quizzes of the magazine variety. They are genuine practice tests from the biggest test publisher in the world, SHL Group plc. This is the real thing. This is what you'll be facing when you apply for a job with virtually any medium-large size company, irrespective of industry, whether private or public sector.

As well as the tests themselves (and the answers) I also indicate the type of job for which each test is commonly used, information on what the assessors are looking for, and tips on how to improve your overall performance within each category of test.

I also include a whole chapter on the different types of **management test** that you will encounter whenever you are invited for interview at a test (or assessment) centre, including the popular *Brainstorm, Scenarios* and *Fastrack* tests used by thousands of organisations around the globe to recruit graduates. **Personality tests** are also covered in great detail, with practice tests to help familiarise yourself with the universally accepted *OPQ 32* questionnaire.

And if that isn't enough, I also include a chapter on **researching** – another vital skill in your armoury, plus a long list of useful books, and internet sites where you can find even more practice material.

My aim in writing this book is to give you both knowledge and experience, not just to survive, but to pass real, live psychometric and management tests with flying colours. Job hunting can be stressful – but not any more!

Andrea Shavick, 2003
www.shavick.com

PART ONE
What are Psychometric Tests?

CHAPTER ONE

What are Psychometric Tests?

Psychometric tests are structured tests, taken in exam-like conditions, which aim to measure objectively a person's ability, or certain aspects of their personality.

Most psychometric tests which measure ability, and virtually all accredited psychometric tests which measure aspects of personality, are devised by occupational psychologists. Their aim is twofold: to provide employers with a reliable method of selecting the best applicants, and to design tests carefully so that they are fair to all applicants.

All psychometric tests, except for personality tests, are strictly timed.

What do psychometric tests measure?

There are many, many different types of psychometric test. A common misconception is that psychometric tests *only* measure personality, but that is not the case.

Some measure your ability to understand the written word, or to reason with numbers. Others measure your ability to solve mechanical problems, or follow instructions accurately, or be able to understand data which is presented in a variety of ways. And then, of course, there are the personality tests, assessing everything from motivation to working preferences.

But psychometric tests cannot measure everything. For example, they can't really measure enthusiasm. Personally, I think that getting in on time every day and making an effort to do your best are to a large extent, determined by how much you enjoy the actual work, how well you get on with your colleagues, and how decent your boss is. Perhaps they should invent a psychometric test for employers!

Who uses psychometric tests?

At the time of writing, well over 95% of the FTSE 100 companies use psychometric testing to select their staff, as do the police, the Civil Service, local authorities, the Armed Forces, the Fire Service and even the National Health Service, financial institutions, retail sector companies, the motor industry, the IT industry, management consultants, airlines, the power industry... the list is endless.

In fact, virtually every large or medium sized organisation in the UK uses psychometric testing as part of their recruitment process, irrespective of industry. Furthermore, the use of psychometric tests is widespread in Europe, Australia and the USA.

And it doesn't matter what level of job you are applying for either. Psychometric tests are used to select all types of staff, everyone from the most junior positions to director level. One thing is certain, if you are looking for a job, you are more than likely to be asked to take a psychometric test.

As to the **why** they are used – see the next chapter.

When will I have to take a psychometric test?

At any stage in the recruitment process, including first contact. These days many employers are so enthusiastic about psychometric tests, they put them on their application forms and websites.

The tests could also pop up later in the process, or even after you've been offered the job when your new boss is deciding exactly where in the organisation to place you.

How many tests will I have to take?

In theory, all psychometric tests given to job applicants should be relevant to the job. You should only have to take, for example, a spatial reasoning test, if the job you are applying for requires good spatial skills.

However, many organisations use verbal, numerical and abstract reasoning tests as a matter of routine, no matter what the job description says. So be prepared to take more than one test.

Where will I have to go to take a psychometric test?

For both ability-type tests and personality questionnaires you could be examined at your potential new employer's office, at an assessment centre, at an employment agency office, or even in the comfort of your own home, using your home computer.

Note: 'Assessment centre' is HR (Human Resources/Personnel) jargon for getting candidates together, either at the employer's premises or an outside location, and subjecting them to an intensive battery of different tests and exercises. These could include role playing, in-tray exercises, group exercises and discussions, presentations and of course, psychometric tests. For more information see Chapter 5 – Assessment Centres, and Chapter 15 – Management Tests.

Note: Some organisations use the phrase 'development centre' instead of assessment centre – they are the same thing.

What format do the tests take?

Most psychometric tests are pencil and paper tests, but a growing number are now designed to be taken sitting at a computer console (see below). However you take the test, the format is almost always that of a multiple-choice questionnaire.

Note: Information on how tests are marked and how to record your answers is given in Chapter 5; Assessment Centres – A Survival Guide.

What about online testing?

Online testing is becoming increasingly common. Instead of being given a pencil and paper test, you take the test on a computer. The questions appear on the screen, and you click your answer choices with the mouse.

Online testing is covered in detail in Chapter 4.

Once I've got the job, will I have to take any more tests?

Quite possibly. Organisations which use tests to recruit often use them later on for internal team selection and career development of individual staff members.

Do other industries use psychometric tests?

Psychometric tests have been used for decades in two main fields other than recruitment. These are career guidance and education.

In career guidance, psychometric tests are used to help individuals gain a better understanding of their own abilities, aptitudes, interests and motivations – obviously very useful information when choosing or changing career. Here, psychometric tests are not used as a selection tool.

However, in education, it's a different ball game. Here, psychometric tests are used by many educational establishments to select the most able pupils. Every year, hundreds of thousands of children as young as 10 years old sit verbal, numerical and abstract reasoning tests in order to gain entrance to the school of their (or their parents') choice. Whole armies of after-hours teachers have for years been making a living tutoring them.

It seems that whether you're job-hunting or school-hunting, when it comes to psychometric tests, familiarisation and practice is the name of the game.

CHAPTER TWO

Why are Psychometric Tests Used?

It makes sense for an employer to find out whether an applicant is capable of doing a job *before* he or she is offered that job, for a number of reasons:

First of all, the whole process of recruiting staff is extremely expensive and time consuming. You might think it's a piece of cake, but to most employers, recruiting is a nightmare, primarily because it's so easy to pick the wrong person. Offering a job which involves figure work to a person who turns out to be unable to use a calculator, would be a disaster. Employing a person in a customer service role who turns out to be incapable of problem solving and bad-tempered into the bargain, could do incalculable damage to a company's standing and reputation.

This might sound obvious, but the truth is that employers have been employing the wrong people for centuries. The difference is, in the 21st century we have tough employment laws which make it virtually impossible for companies to sack people whenever they feel like it. Employee rights, plus the very real risk of being taken to an industrial tribunal make it even more imperative for employers to choose the right people, first time round.

The arrival of the psychometric test has been embraced by many employers because it gives them an additional tool, over and above the traditional methods of interviewing, studying CVs and taking up references. Psychometric tests give employers more confidence in their ability to pick the right people.

Another reason why psychometric tests are used so extensively, especially by large organisations, is because they can be a quick, easy and relatively cheap way of eliminating large numbers of unsuitable candidates early in the recruitment process.

By 'screening out' unsuitable candidates in one fell swoop, the organisation can then concentrate on the remaining candidates in the hope of finding the 'right' people as quickly as possible.

Yet *another* reason why psychometric tests are so popular is because HR people like using them. From their point of view, psychometric tests have many advantages. First of all the use of psychometric testing can reduce their work load considerably. Why interview 100 people, when within an hour, you can whittle this number down to the 30 highest calibre candidates?

You also have to remember that HR staff are human beings, with all the same neuroses and self-doubt the rest of us have. When your job is to recruit staff (and your neck will be on the line if you make a hash of it) it's nice to have a scientific and supposedly fail-safe method at your disposal. What better way to reassure yourself that you've got it right?

If nothing else, psychometric tests give HR people (and anyone else involved in recruiting staff) something to talk about at an interview. This applies especially to personality tests. For example, if the results of your test might indicate you have leadership potential, your interviewer might ask whether you agree with this and possibly ask you to describe situations in which you have used leadership skills. Not only is it useful information for them, it also makes for a more interesting and productive discussion.

Finally, not only are the tests becoming cheaper, there are now more of them to choose from. Test publishers now write psychometric tests for specific jobs, and to an individual company's particular requirements. Tailor-made tests are so common these days, you could apply to a multitude of organisations and never come against the same test twice. You can see the attraction of using a tailor-made test – you'd feel you were getting just the right sort of person your organisation needed. Not only capable of doing the job, but the right personality type to fit seamlessly into your company culture too.

Whatever the reason, the fact is that the psychometric test is a recruitment tool which is very much here to stay.

CHAPTER THREE

Researching Your Chosen Organisation

How can you find out what qualities and abilities an organisation is looking for in its new recruits? Or what it's really like to work for them? How do you decide whether it would be a good career choice for you, or a terrible mistake? The answer is to **research**.

Why research?

Here are some very good reasons:

1. If you get through all the tests you are absolutely, one hundred per cent going to be asked, 'Why do you want to work for us?' Why should any company offer you a job if you cannot give them a convincing answer?

2. Employers are flattered by applicants who take the trouble to find out about their companies, especially since so few of them bother to do it.

3. You can use the information you acquire during your research to enhance your CV and tailor your job application.

4. **As far as psychometric testing is concerned** you'll have advance warning of the type of tests you'll be taking – which is rather useful because then you'll know what to practice.

And if all that doesn't convince you, here's a little anecdote that will: while writing this book I heard about a graduate who sailed through a major car manufacturer's recruitment process, only to be asked in the very final interview for his opinion on their cars. To the interviewer's amazement, the hapless young man proceeded to wax lyrical about a range of cars made by the firm's main competitor! It *always* pays to do your homework!

Now I can almost hear some of you thinking, surely the job ad tells you everything you need to know. Unfortunately, the answer is, it *never* does. It is simply not possible to find out everything about a job, the people, the culture, the ethos, the aims and the successes (or otherwise) of a company from one recruitment advert. For that you need to do some serious digging.

How to research

Here are some great ways to research a company, but be warned. What you discover may help you to land the job, but it could also put you off completely.

1. Experience the product

By this I mean literally take a close look at what the company does. If they are a retailer, visit the stores. If they make a product, have a look at it, examine it, use it. If they offer a service, try it out, or talk to people who have. Look at the company's advertising material, read their leaflets, browse through their catalogues. Get a feel for what they are all about.

2. Find out what their staff think

Many organisations have sections on their web sites featuring interviews with current employees, especially new graduate recruits. And many firms have staff magazines in which they discuss issues relating to the company, or particular industry – ring up their HR (personnel) departments and ask for a copy. The people working in HR departments are usually extremely friendly and will often be happy to talk to you about the organisation and what it's like to work there.

Your tutors may also know of students who have worked there in the past – ask them for contact details and ring for a chat.

University and careers fairs are another opportunity to learn more about a wide range of organisations and chat to members of staff.

3. Find out how successful they are

Don't just assume your chosen company is doing OK, try to find out if they really are. What sort of market share does it have? How successful is the competition? How healthy is its balance sheet? If you have no idea what I'm talking about, ask an accounts or marketing student to give you an opinion! Discovering they're the market leader could make you keener to work there. Uncovering the fact that they're struggling to survive might put you off.

4. Get the job spec and applicant profile

HR departments usually have what they call 'job specs' which list the responsibilities of the actual position, and 'applicant specs' or 'applicant profiles' which describe the qualities and abilities they hope the successful candidate will possess.

Its not always possible to get hold of this information – but what have you got to lose by ringing up and asking for it? As mentioned above, HR staff are usually very happy to talk to you about the companies they work for, and even if you can't get the 'person spec' you should be able to pick up plenty of other valuable information to help you in your application.

Note: Many companies state the personal qualities and abilities they look for in their graduates on their web sites.

5. Study the web site

This is the quickest way to discover what it's like to work for a specific organisation. Not only will you get the official 'blurb' on the product or service they offer, you should also be able to pick up a huge amount of information on their recruitment process.

To find any company website, either use a search engine, or try www.kellysearch.com which lists contact details, descriptions and links to thousands of companies.

Most big companies have *recruitment* flagged up on their home page, but if they don't then try clicking on *company information* instead. Once you get past the hype about how wonderful it is to work there, you'll probably see links to various different types of recruitment, ie experienced professional, apprentice, and graduate careers. From there it's just a matter of exploring. All you need is the time to do it.

Here's a selection of the sort of information you can access by studying the recruitment pages of a typical big-company web site:

♦ The hoops you'll have to jump through in order to get a job, ie online application, personality and ability tests, telephone interview, assessment event, more psychometric tests, final interview.
♦ From what degree disciplines they recruit graduates from.

- How many graduates they take.
- Whether they consider industry experience important.
- The personal qualities and abilities they look for in their graduates.
- Dates and venues of university and career fairs they are visiting (usually between October and December).
- Start dates for graduate programmes, summer placements and longer term placements, plus deadlines for applications.
- How long graduate programmes last.
- Whether there is a probationary period for graduates on the programme.
- Information on fast-track graduate career progression.
- Whether they operate mentor schemes.
- Whether they will consider candidates who graduated in previous academic years.
- Whether they offer relocation assistance.
- Whether it's possible to move between any of their associated companies.
- Whether you can switch business areas after completing your graduate programme.
- Whether they support graduates studying for external qualifications.
- Whether they sponsor higher degrees.
- The career development and training they offer.
- The location of their offices, manufacturing plants, outlets and main recruiting sites.
- How much they pay.
- What the hours are like ... and much, much more.

Note: The company FAQ (frequently asked questions page) is usually a good place to start researching. And as mentioned above, company web sites often feature interviews with recent graduate recruits.

Then sit back and ask yourself whether it all fits in with your expectations. Do you still like what you see? Would you feel proud to work for them? Are you still as enthusiastic about the idea as you were before you began your research? If you value your happiness, these are vitally important questions that need to be asked.

If you *are* still interested, then the next thing you need to do is look on the site for details of the company's recruitment process, which more often than not will include an online psychometric test. Online testing is covered in the next chapter.

CHAPTER FOUR

Online Testing

What are online tests?

An online test is simply a psychometric test you take sitting at a computer console via the Internet. Instead of paper and pencil, it's all mouse action.

Within a few seconds of finishing the test, your score (for an ability test) or the analysis of your personality is emailed to the examiner.

What type of tests can be taken online?

Personality questionnaires, competency questionnaires, and virtually all ability-type tests. The only type of tests which are difficult to administer via the Internet are the management tests which job applicants do not usually encounter until they are invited to attend an assessment centre appointment (the next chapter explains all about this).

How long are online tests?

Most online tests are fairly short, and certainly far shorter than the tests you'll be expected to take if you visit an assessment centre or the recruiting company's premises.

When will I have to take an online test?

Usually right at the very beginning of the recruitment process. Online tests are used to sift applicants at the earliest stage and pinpoint those individuals who may be suitable.

Where will I have to go to take an online test?

Only as far as the nearest computer connected to the Internet. Candidates take online tests at home, in career offices, in employment agencies, on tropical beaches...

What are the advantages of online testing?

For you, it means no worries about getting anywhere on time, and no worries about what to wear. Since you can take an online test any time of the day or night, you won't need to skip any classes, or even get dressed! Plus, you should find out if the organisation is interested in taking your application any further within a few minutes, which is a million times better than waiting for them to send you a letter.

The obvious advantage to the employer is that the candidate doesn't have come into the office. They can take the test at university, in a career office, at a recruitment agency, or even in the comfort of their own home. Instead of spending money 'entertaining' large numbers of candidates, the employer can whittle down the numbers without having to lift a finger. Another advantage for international firms is that they can test candidates anywhere in the world.

How does online testing work?

- Simply surf to the web site of the company you are interested in applying to.

- Look for a link through to 'recruitment' or if that isn't available, click on 'company information' which normally includes the relevant part of the site.

- Skip through the blurb about how wonderful it is to work there (although see Chapter 3 on researching companies) and click on the area of work you're interested in.

- Follow the instructions on screen, typing your details in the relevant boxes. If the application form asks for a lot of very detailed information, print out a copy and consider your answers carefully before filling in the real thing online.

- Once you've registered your details and/or filled in the application form, you will usually receive an acknowledgement and then the assessment process will begin.

- When you get to the test, read the questions carefully and click your answer choices with the mouse. **Work quickly because most tests are set to time out after a certain period of time.** This is to prevent you consulting your dictionary, your physics manual, or your best mate – more on this below.

- Make sure you answer all the questions. If there are any you really can't do, take an educated guess. Never leave a question unanswered.

- Within a few seconds of finishing the test, your score (for an ability test) or the analysis of your personality is emailed to the examiner. Tests are usually marked automatically, so it's very fast. Many employers will let you know the result within a few days, or even immediately.

Note: Even if you apply for a job in writing or on the telephone, you may still be directed to an online test before you can progress further with your application. Some companies prefer to give you a date and time for an online test once you've made contact.

For examples of the psychometric tests go to Part Two of this book.

Cheating – is it possible?

Tempting isn't it? If your prospective employer can't actually see you, how do they know it's *you* taking the test and not your genius of a best mate? Or that she isn't sitting next to you helpfully prompting you with the answers?

The answer is, they can't. However, if cheating does succeed in getting you further along the recruitment road, the chances are that you'll be found out. How? Well, practically all companies who use online testing *retest* successful candidates further down the line, either at an assessment centre or at interview. If your score turns out to be a lot worse than your online test, they'll know why. Sorry about that.

So be warned – your online test will *not* be the only psychometric test you will have to take. HR people are not stupid. Knowing how easy it is to cheat in the online test, many companies deliberately pick a selection of candidates, and with them safely inside the assessment centre or company premises, they spring the same test on them! If you cheated the first time, you'll get rumbled.

More on the perils of test cheating are explained in Chapter 14 on Personality Tests.

CHAPTER FIVE

Assessment Centres – A Survival Guide

Thousands of people visit assessment centres every year. This chapter is full of tips to help you feel good, boost your confidence, get you prepared and organised, and generally help you to survive the day itself.

Note: This chapter does *not* contain the actual tests themselves. For that you'll need Part Two of this book, which includes:

◆ **ability tests**
◆ **personality tests**
◆ **management tests.**

What is an assessment centre?

Assessment Centre is HR (Human Resources/Personnel) jargon for getting a group of prospective candidates together, either at the employer's premises or an outside location, and subjecting them to an intensive battery of different tests and exercises as part of the recruitment process. Sometimes the term 'development centre' is used instead.

When will I get invited for an assessment centre appointment?

Not until you are well into the recruitment process and have already passed through the initial screening process. In other words, not until the organisation in question is seriously interested in you.

What type of tests will I have to sit at an assessment centre?

The average assessment centre (if there is such a thing as an *average* one) will include several ability-type psychometric tests, a personality questionnaire and at least one interview. If you're going for a management or trainee management position, then you're quite likely to have to take several management tests, such as the ones detailed in Chapter 15.

For detailed information about the actual tests and practice material, go to Part Two.

Will all the tests be paper and pencil tests?

Not necessarily. Many companies sit candidates down in front of computers or give them pocket PCs to take their psychometric tests on. Management-type tests generally follow completely different formats altogether.

What will the selectors be looking for?

A range of qualities, including good communication and interpersonal skills, listening skills, confidence, the ability to work well with other people, decision-making skills among other things ... plus a high standard of achievement on the psychometric tests.

How long will my assessment centre appointment take?

An assessment centre visit usually takes the best part of a whole day, but sometimes candidates are asked to stay overnight and sit more tests the next day. Talk about tough...

Preparing for the visit

By far the most useful thing you can do to bolster your self-confidence is to get as much information as possible about the sort of tests you'll be up against (and the pass marks) in advance.

Some companies automatically tell you exactly what to expect during your assessment centre visit. If they don't, then you need to take the initiative. Simply call their HR department (or your prospective new boss) and ask for more information. Ask about the tests and exercises you'll be taking, and whether they can send you any sample material.

If you get the opportunity, ask about the job, and the organisation as well. Personnel managers are usually, by the very nature of their jobs, friendly and approachable, and it's extremely unlikely that they'll object to helping you. So long as you are polite and professional, there is no reason why you shouldn't be successful every time.

Not only have you nothing to lose, phoning could give you a clear advantage in more ways than one. If you know what to expect you'll be better prepared, not to mention more relaxed, and also, very few of the other candidates will do it. From the employer's point of view, you will have become a candidate who is showing interest – exactly the sort of person they want.

Other things to do in advance are:

Get directions

Make sure you've got the exact address, and good directions. And find out which bus or train to take.

Get organised

Decide what you're going to wear *before* the day in question (see **Look smart**, below). I nearly missed an interview once because I spent so long trying on different outfits. For some strange reason, time speeds up considerably when you're late. Shine your shoes, sort out your briefcase, find your glasses, and if you're going to be staying overnight, pack your overnight bag... very carefully. The last thing you'll want is to discover you've forgotten your toothbrush.

Relax

Laughter is a great cure for nervous tension, so perhaps rent an amusing DVD or go and see a film the night before. But not the late show – you'll need a good night's sleep. Alternatively, get some exercise and follow it up with a long soak in the bath.

On the day itself

Eat a good breakfast

Include simple sugars (fruit juice) and complex carbohydrates (toast or cereal) and possibly some protein (milk, eggs, cheese, meat). This will keep your blood sugar stable and your energy levels up. Make sure you eat and drink during the day too – don't starve yourself.

Look smart

One of the best ways to boost your self-confidence is to look smart. If you look good and you know it, you'll feel good too. Treat your assessment centre visit as if you're going along to an interview, and dress accordingly. Even if you're absolutely certain that you're not going to have a face-to-face interview or make a presentation, it's still important to make an effort with your appearance. You'll feel better for it too.

Over-estimate your journey time

If you're driving, plan the route and allow extra time for tractors, jack-knifed lorries and those awful temporary traffic lights which seem to materialise overnight. The same applies to bus and rail journeys. If a bus or train is going to cancelled, it'll be yours.

There's another reason why arriving punctually is essential. If you are being tested alongside other candidates, you will most likely to have been given a start time for the tests. If you arrive late, everyone else will have already begun and the organisation will be reluctant to disturb them by allowing you into the room. To put it bluntly – arrive late and you probably won't be allowed to take the test at all.

Besides, think about the impression your lateness will make on your prospective employer. They'll think, 'If he's late today, think how terrible his timekeeping will be once he's got the job.'

Smile

When you do arrive, always be polite and friendly. Smile, and people will smile back at you. You'll look confident, even if your knees are shaking.

Be friendly

Make an effort to get to know the other candidates. Taking tests, being interviewed, giving presentations and problem-solving alongside other applicants is very stressful, but be assured everyone else will be feeling as nervous as you.

So make it easier for yourself by being sociable, friendly and likeable. Chatting to the other candidates and the people from the recruiting company will not only help to overcome your nerves, it will help your chances of landing the job too. Passing the tests is one thing, but you'll never get the job unless they also actually *like* you.

Be professional

Being friendly is one thing, but don't overdo it. If you're going to be staying overnight at the assessment centre, remember you're there to land a job, not seduce the administrator or prop up the bar all night.

Stay cool

And what if your knees are still shaking? Here are a few relaxation exercises that will help you handle the stress. With a little practice, you'll be able to use them anywhere; in the car, on the bus, in the exam room...

1. Breathing exercise
Breathe in slowly to really fill your lungs. Hold your breath for three seconds, then slowly breathe out through your mouth. As you breathe out, imagine all the tension and stress flowing out with the air. Repeat two or three times.

2. Tension release exercise
Tense the muscle groups one by one, and then relax them. Begin with your feet: screw up your toes as tightly as possible and hold for three or four seconds. Then slowly relax. Continue upwards through your body, working your legs, your stomach, your hands, your arms, your shoulders and even your face.

3. Tension release exercise number 2
This is a good last-minute exercise to use while you're waiting to be called into the test room, or just before you give a presentation. Simply go to the bathroom, make sure no one can see you (you do *not* want an audience for this) and make yourself shake like a jelly. I

mean really, physically shake your whole body for at least 20 seconds. Pretend you're auditioning for a low-budget horror movie. Then stop, take a few slow, deep breaths, and off you go. I guarantee you'll suddenly feel incredibly calm and composed and ready for anything.

Surviving the tests

Here are a few tips for when you're sitting in an exam hall, about to take a psychometric test:

Listen carefully

When you are taking psychometric tests, or any sort of test for that matter, you *must* listen very carefully to the test administrator's instructions. Pay particular attention to what they say about the end of the test. **Unlike academic exams, the administrator may not be allowed to warn candidates that time's nearly up.**

Ask questions first

If there is anything about the test instructions you do not understand, or you have any other problem at all, then the time to ask is before it starts. Once the clock is ticking no interruptions will be allowed. Although I guess it's acceptable to tell the administrator that half your test paper is missing. And it wouldn't be the first time.

Check out the paper

Instead of plunging straight into the test, have a quick look though the paper so you can see what you're up against. Is there a separate answer sheet? How many questions are there? How many different sections? Plenty of people have sat smugly in an exam room congratulating themselves on their speed only to discover, right at the last minute, that they've missed the last page. That really is a horrible feeling, but by checking out the paper first you won't have a problem.

Pace yourself

Pacing yourself is all about working through the paper at the right speed. Too fast and your accuracy will suffer. Too slow and you'll run out of time.

Once you've looked at the test paper, try to estimate how much time you have to answer each question, for example 50 questions in 25 minutes equals 30 seconds each. Once you've done this you'll know that after 10 minutes you should have tackled around 20 questions, and after 20 minutes you should have tackled around 40 questions and so on. As you work through the paper, check your progress from time to time. This should ensure you never get too far behind, and also reassure you that you're doing OK.

Some people even advise scribbling the desired 'finish time' for each section right there on the test paper to remind you to check the clock as you work through the test. Personally I think this takes up too much valuable time, but it could be a trick that works for you.

Note: Sometimes the ability-type tests get harder as you go along, so consider leaving more time for the later questions.

One tricky situation that can occur is when you come up against a question that you simply cannot answer. If you only have around 30 seconds per question, you can see that spending 10 minutes on one of them is a bad idea. So if you get stuck, don't give yourself a hard time, simply give it up and move on. If you make a tiny mark next to the unanswered question (or ring the question number) you'll be able to see at a glance which questions still need tackling. If you have any time at the end, you can go back and try again.

Read the questions

Read each question carefully so you know exactly what information you are being asked for. This might sound totally obvious, but when you're under stress it's very tempting to rush and not bother to check what you're being asked to do. Many people (myself included) are so used to scanning through chunks of text at high speed, they find reading every single word with concentration incredibly difficult. So slow down and concentrate.

Work through the questions in order

Some people skip through test papers looking for questions they know they'll be able to answer easily. The trouble with this is that it wastes time, it's better to work through the paper in order. As I explained above, if you can't answer a question, mark it and move on to the next one.

Record your answers as instructed

Psychometric tests usually come in a multiple-choice format. This means you will be given four or five possible answer choices for each question. Once you have decided which is the correct one, mark the corresponding box or circle on the answer sheet accordingly. An example of how to do this will usually given at the beginning of the paper.

It is vitally important that you follow these directions precisely. If you are asked to fill in the box or circle, **fill it in completely**. Don't just make a little squiggle inside it, or tick it or put a cross through it.

Most psychometric tests are marked either by computers using a technique called optical marking, or the test administrators using an 'answer grid' which they lay over the answer sheet.

Either way, if you record your answers in the correct way, the computer (or test administrator) will be able to 'read' them. If you don't, you'll lose points – even if your answers are correct.

The same goes for the number of answers required. If you are asked to mark one circle, mark only one circle. If you mark two, the computer or test administrator will not know which is your intended correct answer, and you'll lose a mark, even if one of the answers is correct.

The same advice also goes for psychometric tests taken on a computer, although generally the program will not allow you to click more than one answer choice.

Concentrate

Many people find it difficult to concentrate intensely for long periods of time. It isn't easy to block out everything around you and work non-stop for up to an hour without a break.

Even if you are working in a quiet room without disturbance, your mind can start to play tricks on you. I find that I begin well but after a few minutes my mind starts to wander. I begin to think about virtually anything else in the world other than the test. What shall I have for supper? Where did I put my train ticket? Is everyone else miles ahead of me? Why won't the guy in front stop sniffing?

The best way to combat this is to take a very short break. Sit up straight, shut your eyes and take two or three long slow breaths (see the breathing exercise above, under **Stay**

cool). Or try keeping your eyes open and focusing at a point in the distance for about ten seconds.

Use tried and tested exam techniques

◆ Try to work out the correct answer before looking at any of the answer choices. That way, even if you can't come up with a definite answer, you'll be able to make an educated guess.

◆ Narrow your choices by immediately eliminating answers you can see are incorrect.

◆ If you think a question could be a 'trick' question, think again. Psychometric tests are always straightforward, there are never questions intended to deceive. It could be that you're reading too much into the question; instead try to take it at face value.

◆ Only change your answer if you are absolutely sure you have answered incorrectly. First answers are usually the correct ones.

◆ Keep working through the paper at a steady pace, keeping an eye on the clock.

Don't panic

You're almost out of time and you've got that horrible sinking feeling that says, 'Help! I'm not going to finish!' – don't panic. Instead, reassure yourself with these facts:

1. You don't have to score 100% to pass. In fact, many organisations set the 'pass' level of their psychometric tests as low as 50%. The whole point of the test is to eliminate candidates who are totally hopeless, so they can concentrate on the rest of you.

2. Many ability-type tests are not designed to be finished in the time set. Giving you more questions than you can reasonably cope with in the allotted time is a deliberate ploy. Taking a psychometric test is meant to be stressful! Afterwards, if any of the other candidates boast about finishing 15 minutes ahead of the rest of the room – they're probably lying.

3. Finally, remember that if you are taking a personality test – there are no wrong answers. With a maths test there is definitely a right and a wrong answer, but with a personality test there isn't any such thing.

Getting feedback

In theory you should always be offered feedback on your assessment centre performance, but in practice it doesn't always happen. However there's nothing to stop you contacting the company's HR department a few days later and asking.

What about the tests themselves?

For detailed information about the tests you will be taking, plus all the practice material, see Part Two of this book.

What about management-type tests, group exercises, presentations and role plays?

These are all explained in Chapter 15 – Management Tests.

PART TWO
The Practice Tests

Introduction

Everyone is different. All the people you know have different skills. Some of them are fluent communicators. Some of them have great technical ability. Some are creative. Some are innovative. Some of them can solve complicated number problems quicker than ordinary mortals eat chocolate.

But here's the catch: nobody is good at everything. Almost all of us have areas in which we are not very adept. As a writer, my ability to communicate in writing is pretty reasonable, (well, my mum thinks so anyway). But ask me to change a light bulb, or calculate my car's petrol consumption and I'm lost.

The reason I'm telling you this is because what follows is a vast selection of practice psychometric tests used to recruit graduates. However that doesn't mean that just because you are a graduate (or nearly one) that you'll sail through the entire book without any problems. Some you'll find easy, but some will definitely give you a hard time. Most of the technical tests fox me, even with the answers right in front of my nose!

So whatever you do, don't despair if you find some of the questions (or even whole sections) difficult. You certainly won't be the only one. Remember, **the whole point of this book is to familiarise yourself with the different types of test and give yourself the chance to practice, thereby helping you improve your performance.**

Note: Wherever you have difficulty with the questions, analysing them with the answers in front of you should make things clearer.

How the practice tests are arranged

The different types of psychometric test are arranged in separate chapters. The ability-type tests come first, followed by combination tests, then personality questionnaires, and finally a chapter on management tests. This one includes tests and exercises you might be expected to do at an assessment centre.

At the end of each chapter there is a section dedicated to helping you improve your performance ... and the answers of course, where applicable.

How to get the best out of this book

To get the best out this book, treat the practice tests as if you were taking them in a live interview. In other words, sit somewhere quiet, without distractions, and work as quickly and as accurately, and with as much concentration as you can. If you find it tough going don't worry, the more you try, the easier it will become.

Record your answer choices in pencil by filling in completely the appropriate circles on the Answer Sheet (there is one for each test with the exception of several of the management-type tests). This will familiarise you with the technique for recording your answers.

Time limits

Almost all the practice tests have suggested time limits. Set the clock, and attempt as many questions as you can in the time allowed, but don't worry if you can't complete all the questions. In the real world, *psychometric tests always have more questions than most people can handle*. It's a deliberate ploy to put you under pressure, to see how you work when under stress. Besides, working under a time constraint is good experience in itself.

Of course, there's nothing to stop you giving yourself more time, or attempting the questions as many times as you like – even after you've checked the answers.

Concentrating

You can also work through each test in its entirety, if for no other reason than to train your brain to concentrate. Remember that these tests are **practice** tests – when you apply for a job, the psychometric tests you'll take will generally be longer, with more questions. Getting used to concentrating for longer periods of time will stand you in good stead and give you an advantage over the other candidates.

If you want to practise a particular type of test, the following list will help you locate the one you want quickly:

Numerical Reasoning Tests

Abstract Reasoning Tests

Spatial Reasoning Tests

Mechanical Comprehension Tests

Fault Diagnosis Tests

Accuracy Tests

Remember – familiarisation and practice is the name of the game! Good luck.

CHAPTER SIX

Verbal Reasoning

Verbal reasoning tests are multiple-choice tests which measure your ability to reason with words. They are widely used in recruitment to select staff, simply because the ability to understand the written word is an essential skill for most jobs.

The simplest verbal reasoning tests assess your basic language skills: spelling, vocabulary and understanding of grammar. You are usually presented with four or five different words, or groups of words, and asked to pick the ones which:

✓ are spelt correctly
✓ are spelt incorrectly
✓ do not belong in the group
✓ mean the same
✓ mean the opposite
✓ best complete a sentence
✓ best fill the gaps in a sentence.

Here's a couple of examples:

Choose the words which **best** complete the following sentences:

All employees should...............from such a training scheme.
A. result   B. credit   C. succeed   D. enrol   E. benefit

The..............is..............if you do not pay on time.
A. pollicy   B. pollicy   C. polisy   D. polisy   E. none of these
   forfieted   forfeated   forfieted   forfeated

What's being tested is your vocabulary, spelling and grammatical skills, pretty basic stuff for a graduate. The answers, of course, are both E.

Analogies are also popular. Artist is to painting, as author is to:

A. keyboard
B. publisher
C. book
D. bicycle

What's being tested here is your ability to recognise relationships between words. If an artist *creates* a painting, what might an author create? The correct answer is C.

There are lots of examples of this type of test in my first psychometric testing book, *Passing Psychometric Tests* (also published by How To Books).

Graduate level verbal reasoning tests on the other hand, are slightly harder. They not only measure language skills, they examine your ability to make sense of, and logically evaluate, the written word. These tests are often called **critical reasoning** tests, but in essence they are comprehension exercises. In each case you are required to read a short text, or passage and then answer questions about it.

However, unlike the comprehension exercises that you did in school, where the answers were obvious so long as you read the text carefully enough, critical reasoning tests generally require a little more brain power.

You are often asked to decide whether a statement is true or false, or impossible to verify, *given the information contained in the passage*. This last phrase is very important. Not only are you being forced to think very carefully about what you have read, you must endeavour not to make any assumptions about it. You must answer the question using only the given information – something which is surprisingly difficult to do if you have any knowledge of (or an opinion on) the subject matter in question. Remember, it is only your ability to understand and make logical deductions from the passage that is being tested, not your knowledge of the subject matter.

The vocabulary and subject of the passage are often similar to those encountered in the actual job for which you are applying. For example, if you are applying for a technical job in IT, then any verbal reasoning test you encounter is quite likely to include the language, vocabulary and jargon prevalent in that industry.

All verbal reasoning psychometric tests are strictly timed, and *every single question will have one, and only one correct answer.*

In this chapter

In this chapter there are 5 different graduate level verbal reasoning practice tests for you to try, of varying difficulty. Before each one I've indicated for what sort of job, or area of work you might be expected to take that particular type of test.

At the end of the chapter there is section entitled **Verbal Reasoning Tests – How To Improve Your Performance** which is intended to help you do just that across the whole range of verbal reasoning tests. Included in this section are some hints on tackling the questions themselves. If you have a problem with any of the questions then hopefully the advice contained in this sections will get you back on track. Remember however that all of us have strengths and weaknesses, and everyone will have some difficulty with some of the tests in this book.

Test 1 Verbal Reasoning

This test measures your ability to evaluate the logic of written information. It is designed for staff who need to understand and interpret written material with a technical context.

This type of test is designed for the selection, development and promotion of staff working in Information Technology and is suitable for applicants with A levels to graduate qualification or equivalent.

Instructions: In this test you are given two passages, each of which is followed by several statements. You are required to evaluate the statements in the light of the information or opinions contained in the passage and select your answer according to the rules below:

Mark circle A if the statement is patently **true**, or follows logically *given the information in the passage*.

Mark circle B if the statement is patently **untrue**, or if the opposite follows logically, *given the information in the passage*.

Mark circle C if you **cannot say** whether the statement is true or follows logically *without further information*.

Indicate your answer each time by filling in completely the appropriate circle on the answer sheet.

Time guideline: See how many questions you can complete in 5 minutes.

Among the useful features available on this computer system is the **Notebk** feature. The **Notebk** feature organises lists of information in a record format. Its most obvious use is for lists of names, phone numbers and addresses but many other applications can be defined. One of the biggest advantages of using **Notebk** is that the files are stored in a format that can be used directly by other features. This means that files do not have to be converted or altered in any way.

---

1   The **Notebk** feature can only be used to organise lists of names, phone numbers and addresses.

2   If users wish to use **Notebk** files with other features, they do not need to alter the files.

3   The **Notebk** feature enables the user to instantly update lists of names and addresses.

Software engineering is an approach to the improvement of system productivity. In most circumstances, it has a modest impact on the productivity of the system during the initial development stage. However, systems developed using software engineering techniques have substantially lower maintenance costs and higher reliability.

4   Lower maintenance costs can be expected if the system used was developed using software engineering techniques.

5   Systems developed with these techniques are more likely to break down.

6   Software engineering is a widely used methodology when developing new systems.

Test 1 Answer Sheet

	A	B	C
1	Ⓐ	Ⓑ	Ⓒ
2	Ⓐ	Ⓑ	Ⓒ
3	Ⓐ	Ⓑ	Ⓒ
4	Ⓐ	Ⓑ	Ⓒ
5	Ⓐ	Ⓑ	Ⓒ
6	Ⓐ	Ⓑ	Ⓒ

Test 2 Verbal Evaluation

This test measures your ability to understand and evaluate the logic of various kinds or argument.

This type of test is often used to assess reasoning skills at administrative, supervisory and junior management levels and for a wide range of jobs, including office supervisors, senior personal assistants, junior managers and management trainees.

Instructions: In this test you are required to evaluate each statement in the light of the passage and select your answer according to the rules below:

Mark circle A if the statement follows logically from *the information or opinions contained in the passage*.

Mark circle B if the statement is obviously false from *the information or opinions contained in the passage*.

Mark circle C if you cannot say whether the statement is true or false *without further information*.

Indicate your answer each time by filling in completely the appropriate circle on the answer sheet.

Time guideline: See how many questions you can complete in 5 minutes.

> Many organisations find it beneficial to employ students during the summer. Permanent staff often wish to take their own holidays over this period. Furthermore, it is not uncommon for companies to experience peak workloads in the summer and so require extra staff. Summer employment also attracts students who may return as well qualified recruits to an organisation when they have completed their education. Ensuring that the students learn as much as possible about the organisation encourages their interest in working on a permanent basis. Organisations pay students on a fixed rate without the usual entitlement to paid holidays or sick leave.

1   It is possible that permanent staff who are on holiday can have their work carried out by students.

2   Students in summer employment are given the same paid holiday benefit as permanent staff.

3   Students are subject to the organisation's standard disciplinary and grievance procedures.

4   Some companies have more work to do in summer when students are available for vacation work.

Most banks and building societies adopt a 'no smoking' policy in customer areas in their branches. Plaques and stickers are displayed in these areas to draw attention to this policy. The notices are worded in a 'customer friendly' manner, though a few customers may feel their personal freedom of choice is being infringed. If a customer does ignore a notice, staff are tolerant and avoid making a great issue of the situation. In fact, the majority of customers now expect a 'no smoking' policy in premises of this kind. After all, such a policy improves the pleasantness of the customer facilities and also lessens fire risk.

5   'No smoking' policies have mainly been introduced in response to customer demand.

6   All banks and building societies now have a 'no smoking' policy.

7   There is no conflict of interest between a 'no smoking' policy and personal freedom of choice for all.

8   A no-smoking policy is in line with most customers' expectations in banks and building societies.

Test 2 Answer Sheet

	A	B	C
1	Ⓐ	Ⓑ	Ⓒ
2	Ⓐ	Ⓑ	Ⓒ
3	Ⓐ	Ⓑ	Ⓒ
4	Ⓐ	Ⓑ	Ⓒ
5	Ⓐ	Ⓑ	Ⓒ
6	Ⓐ	Ⓑ	Ⓒ
7	Ⓐ	Ⓑ	Ⓒ
8	Ⓐ	Ⓑ	Ⓒ

Test 3 Technical Understanding

This test measures your ability to understand a written passage containing the type of material likely to be found in a typical technical setting.

This type of test is often used in the selection and development of individuals in technically or practically orientated jobs. You might find it slightly easier than some of the other tests.

Instructions: You are required to read the passage carefully, then, using the information provided, answer the questions which follow. Indicate your answer each time by filling in completely the appropriate circle on the answer sheet.

Time guideline: See how many questions you can complete in 2 minutes.

Company van use/allocation codes

Three codes exist for company vans:

001 – possess company van with full expenses paid
002 – possess company van with partial expenses paid
003 – has the facility to borrow a company van
004 – does not have the facility to borrow a company van

All senior members have 001 codes; 002 codes are automatically given to non-senior members after 2 years of relevant service and 003 codes exist for members who have not been with the company for two years but whose jobs include a high driving element. People with 004 codes tend to be those without a driving licence or individuals who rarely have the need for a van.

Test 3 SHL Group Plc 2003. SHL and OPQ are registered trademarks of SHL Group plc which are registered in the United Kingdom and other countries.

1   Which code would a senior member with two years service have?

A) 001.

B) 002.

C) 003.

D) 004.

2   Members who only have 1 year of service but spend a large part of their time driving, would have which code?

A) 001.

B) 002.

C) 003.

D) 004.

3   Which facility is unique to code 002?

A) The company van.

B) Partial expenses.

C) Full expenses.

D) A borrowing facility.

4   An individual who has worked for the company for three years but who does not drive would be given what code?

A) 001.

B) 002.

C) 003.

D) 004.

Test 3 Answer Sheet

	A	B	C	D
1	Ⓐ	Ⓑ	Ⓒ	Ⓓ
2	Ⓐ	Ⓑ	Ⓒ	Ⓓ
3	Ⓐ	Ⓑ	Ⓒ	Ⓓ
4	Ⓐ	Ⓑ	Ⓒ	Ⓓ

Test 4 Verbal Evaluation

This test measures your ability to understand and evaluate the logic of fairly complex written arguments. This type of test is often used in the selection and development of individuals over a wide range of sales or customer service roles.

Instructions: The test consists of a series of passages, each of which is followed by several statements. You are required to evaluate each statement given the information or opinions contained in the passage, and select your answer according to the rules below:

Mark circle A if the statement is true given *the information or opinions contained in the passage.*

Mark circle B if the statement is obviously false given *the information or opinions contained in the passage.*

Mark circle C if you cannot say whether the statement is true or false *without further information.*

Indicate your answer each time by filling in completely the appropriate circle on the answer sheet.

Time guideline: See how many questions you can answer in 4 minutes.

The Osprey hotel chain yesterday confirmed plans to introduce a range of theme restaurants, amid speculation that it is facing severe financial difficulties. The concept was tested out in the flagship hotel during a three month period last summer. During that period the increase in average charge per head and the number of meals served surpassed all expectations. Competitors view the programme as the last feasible attempt to prevent this household name from becoming a distant memory.

---

1. The Osprey chain is about to close down.

2. Competing hotel chains believe that should this project fail, no other remedial action would save the company.

3. Estimates concerning the impact of the theme restaurants upon sales in the flagship hotel were accurate.

4. Osprey is a well known hotel chain.

Despite their aesthetic landscaping, ease of access and generous parking, out-of-town business parks have not turned out to be the attractive proposition that speculative developers had hoped. Their polished appearance and spaciousness have failed to compensate for limited provision of basic infrastructure such as shops, banks and leisure facilities as less scrupulous developers reneged on earlier promises or struggled with cash flow problems and other difficulties. It is thought that an expansion of home working, relying on advanced communication systems and technology, would make visits to smaller head offices situated in the heart of town centres more acceptable.

5. Proximity to retail outlets is seen as an important issue when evaluating office locations.

6. The continued popularity of business parks will be reinforced by new technology.

7. Cash flow is the main problem for speculative developers.

8. In certain circumstances, there have been discrepancies between the original plans and the finished business park.

Test 4 Answer Sheet

	A	B	C
1	Ⓐ	Ⓑ	Ⓒ
2	Ⓐ	Ⓑ	Ⓒ
3	Ⓐ	Ⓑ	Ⓒ
4	Ⓐ	Ⓑ	Ⓒ
5	Ⓐ	Ⓑ	Ⓒ
6	Ⓐ	Ⓑ	Ⓒ
7	Ⓐ	Ⓑ	Ⓒ
8	Ⓐ	Ⓑ	Ⓒ

Test 5 Verbal Test

This test measures your ability to evaluate the logic of written information. This type of test is frequently used to select graduates over a wide range of industries.

Instructions: In this test you are given two passages, each of which is followed by several statements. You are required to evaluate the statements in the light of the information or opinions contained in the passage and select your answer according to the rules given below:

Mark circle A if the statement is patently **true**, or follows logically *given the information or opinions contained in the passage.*

Mark circle B if the statement is patently **untrue**, or if the opposite follows logically, *given the information or opinions contained in the passage.*

Mark circle C if you **cannot say** whether the statement is true or untrue or follows logically *without further information.*

Indicate your answer each time by filling in completely the appropriate circle on the answer sheet.

Time guideline: There is no official time guideline for this practice test, however, try to work through the questions as quickly as you can.

The big economic difference between nuclear and fossil-fuelled power stations is that nuclear reactors are more expensive to build and decommission, but cheaper to run. So disputes over the relative efficiency of the two systems revolve not just around the prices of coal and uranium today and tomorrow, but also around the way in which future income should be compared with current income.

---

1   The main difference between nuclear and fossil-fuelled power stations is an economic one.

2   The price of coal is not relevant to discussions about the relative efficiency of nuclear reactors.

3   If nuclear reactors were cheaper to build and decommission than fossil-fuelled power stations, they would definitely have the economic advantage.

At any given moment we are being bombarded by physical and psychological stimuli competing for our attention. Although our eyes are capable of handling more than 5 millions bits of data per second, our brains are capable of interpreting only about 500 bits per second. With similar disparities between each of the other senses and the brain, it is easy to see that we must select the visual, auditory, or tactile stimuli that we wish to compute at any specific time.

4   Physical stimuli usually win in the competition for our attention.

5   The capacity of the human brain is sufficient to interpret nearly all the stimuli the senses can register under optimum conditions.

6   Eyes are able to cope with the greater input of information than ears.

Test 5 Answer Sheet

	A	B	C
1	Ⓐ	Ⓑ	Ⓒ
2	Ⓐ	Ⓑ	Ⓒ
3	Ⓐ	Ⓑ	Ⓒ
4	Ⓐ	Ⓑ	Ⓒ
5	Ⓐ	Ⓑ	Ⓒ
6	Ⓐ	Ⓑ	Ⓒ

Answers to Verbal Reasoning questions

Test 1 – Verbal Reasoning

	A	B	C
1	Ⓐ	●	Ⓒ
2	●	Ⓑ	Ⓒ
3	Ⓐ	Ⓑ	●
4	●	Ⓑ	Ⓒ
5	Ⓐ	●	Ⓒ
6	Ⓐ	Ⓑ	●

Test 2 – Verbal Evaluation

	A	B	C
1	●	Ⓑ	Ⓒ
2	Ⓐ	●	Ⓒ
3	Ⓐ	Ⓑ	●
4	●	Ⓑ	Ⓒ
5	Ⓐ	Ⓑ	●
6	Ⓐ	●	Ⓒ
7	Ⓐ	●	Ⓒ
8	●	Ⓑ	Ⓒ

Test 3 – Technical Understanding

	A	B	C	D
1	●	Ⓑ	Ⓒ	Ⓓ
2	Ⓐ	Ⓑ	●	Ⓓ
3	Ⓐ	●	Ⓒ	Ⓓ
4	Ⓐ	Ⓑ	Ⓒ	●

Test 4 – Verbal Evaluation

	A	B	C
1	Ⓐ	Ⓑ	●
2	●	Ⓑ	Ⓒ
3	Ⓐ	●	Ⓒ
4	●	Ⓑ	Ⓒ
5	●	Ⓑ	Ⓒ
6	Ⓐ	●	Ⓒ
7	Ⓐ	Ⓑ	●
8	●	Ⓑ	Ⓒ

Test 5 – Verbal Test

	A	B	C
1	Ⓒ	Ⓑ	●
2	Ⓐ	●	Ⓒ
3	●	Ⓑ	Ⓒ
4	Ⓐ	Ⓑ	●
5	Ⓐ	●	Ⓒ
6	Ⓐ	Ⓑ	●

Verbal Reasoning Tests – How To Improve Your Performance

◆ In critical reasoning tests, always read the passage thoroughly. Don't skip through sections, or scan the text at high speed. Reading with understanding requires concentrated effort – not an easy thing to do however good your reading skills. Reread anything of which you are unsure.

◆ Also read the questions very carefully to ensure you understand exactly what you are being asked.

◆ Look at the answer choices and quickly eliminate any you know to be incorrect. Concentrate your energies on deciding between the most likely possibilities.

◆ Think carefully before selecting an answer which includes words like 'always', 'never', 'true', 'false', 'none' and 'all'. These words leave no room for manoeuvre or any exception whatsoever.

◆ Answer the questions using only the given information. Don't let prior knowledge or your opinion on the subject matter influence you. Only your ability to understand and make logical deductions from the passage is being tested.

◆ Verbal reasoning tests demand a high level of concentration, so treat yourself to a break every now and then. Sit up straight, shut your eyes and take a few deep breaths, just for 20 seconds or so. This will calm you down, relax your back and give your eyes and brain a well deserved rest.

To improve general performance in verbal reasoning tests:
◆ Read books and newspapers.
◆ Do verbal problem-solving exercises like crosswords.
◆ If applying for a managerial position, read reports and business journals.
◆ If applying for a technical job, read technical manuals and instruction books.

CHAPTER SEVEN

Numerical Reasoning

Numerical reasoning tests are written, multiple-choice psychometric tests which are used as part of the selection procedure for jobs with any element of figure work. This includes a wide range of jobs, such as those dealing with money, buying, administration, engineering, statistics, analytical science, and any sort of numerical calculations.

In addition, psychometric tests which measure *basic* mathematical ability are also becoming more and more commonplace, simply because firms want to know whether you are numerate or not. So even if you would never dream of applying for a job with any sort of figure work I would recommend you read this chapter.

Numerical reasoning questions can be presented in a variety of different ways, including:

- basic maths
- sequences
- number problems
- numerical estimation problems
- data interpretation using tables, graphs and diagrams

and varying levels of difficulty. Some allow you the use of a calculator, others do not. All numerical reasoning tests are strictly timed, and *every single question will have one, and only one correct answer.*

In this chapter

In this chapter there are 6 different numerical psychometric tests for you to try. Before each one I've indicated for what sort of job, or industry you might be expected to take that particular type of test.

At the end of the chapter there is section entitled **Numerical Reasoning Tests – How To Improve Your Performance** which is intended to help you do just that across the whole range of numerical tests. Included in this section are some hints on tackling the questions themselves. If you have a problem with any of the questions then hopefully the advice contained in this section will get you back on track. Remember, however, that all of us have strengths and weaknesses, and everyone will have some difficulty with some of the tests in this book.

Note: Do not use a calculator unless specifically instructed to do so.

Test 6 Number Series

The following problems are presented as sequences. They measure your ability to reason with numbers. In particular, this test assesses your ability to develop strategies and to recognise the relationships between numbers. Some of the questions are straightforward, others are a little more complicated.

This type of test is designed for the selection, development and promotion of staff working in Information Technology, for example, software engineers, systems analysts, programmers and database administrators, and for any IT job where the recognition of numerical relationships or sequences is important.

It is suitable for applicants with A levels to graduate qualification or equivalent.

Instructions: Each problem in the test consists of a series of numbers on the left of the page, which follow a logical sequence. You are required to choose the next diagram in the series from the five options on the right. Indicate your answer by filling in completely the appropriate circles on the answer sheet. *Do not use a calculator.*

Time guideline: See how many questions you can answer in 5 minutes. Remember to work accurately as well as quickly.

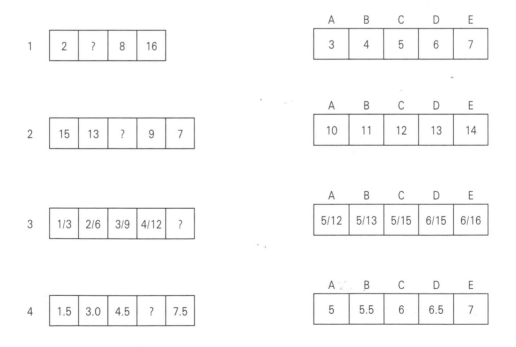

Test 6 SHL Group Plc 2003. SHL and OPQ are registered trademarks of SHL Group plc which are registered in the United Kingdom and other countries.

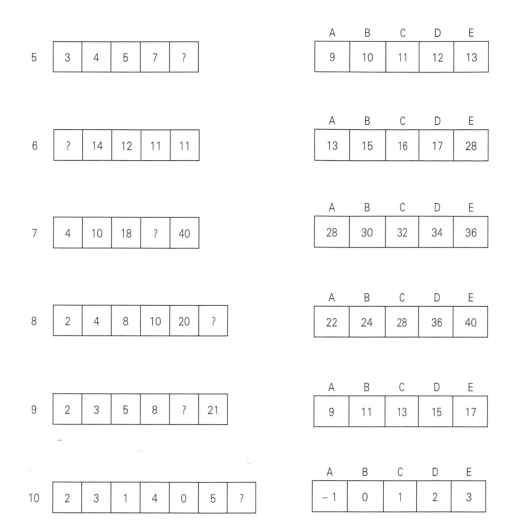

5	3	4	5	7	?

A	B	C	D	E
9	10	11	12	13

6	?	14	12	11	11

A	B	C	D	E
13	15	16	17	28

7	4	10	18	?	40

A	B	C	D	E
28	30	32	34	36

8	2	4	8	10	20	?

A	B	C	D	E
22	24	28	36	40

9	2	3	5	8	?	21

A	B	C	D	E
9	11	13	15	17

10	2	3	1	4	0	5	?

A	B	C	D	E
– 1	0	1	2	3

Test 6 Answer Sheet

	A	B	C	D	E
1	Ⓐ	Ⓑ	Ⓒ	Ⓓ	Ⓔ
2	Ⓐ	Ⓑ	Ⓒ	Ⓓ	Ⓔ
3	Ⓐ	Ⓑ	Ⓒ	Ⓓ	Ⓔ
4	Ⓐ	Ⓑ	Ⓒ	Ⓓ	Ⓔ
5	Ⓐ	Ⓑ	Ⓒ	Ⓓ	Ⓔ
6	Ⓐ	Ⓑ	Ⓒ	Ⓓ	Ⓔ
7	Ⓐ	Ⓑ	Ⓒ	Ⓓ	Ⓔ
8	Ⓐ	Ⓑ	Ⓒ	Ⓓ	Ⓔ
9	Ⓐ	Ⓑ	Ⓒ	Ⓓ	Ⓔ
10	Ⓐ	Ⓑ	Ⓒ	Ⓓ	Ⓔ

Test 7 Numerical Estimation

In this test your ability to quickly *estimate* the answer to a calculation is being assessed. When you take a test of this type, you will not have sufficient time to calculate the exact answer. This skill is very useful in the automated office environment where calculations made by computers often need to be cross-checked.

This type of test is often used at supervisory level, and by a variety of organisations including building societies, banks, retailers and many public sector organisations. The level is fairly basic, but it's a good warm up for Test 8.

Instructions: In this test you are required to *estimate* the order of magnitude of the solution to each calculation and then choose the answer which is nearest to your estimate from the 5 alternative answers.

Indicate your answers by filling in completely the appropriate boxes on the answer sheet. *Do not use a calculator.*

Time guideline: There is no official time guideline for this practice test. However, because in a real live test situation you will not be given sufficient time to calculate the exact answer, work as quickly as you possibly can.

1   $19 + 27$

A	B	C	D	E
56	32	46	4.6	306

2   20% of 56

A	B	C	D	E
280	11.2	28	112	2.8

3   $72 - 18$

A	B	C	D	E
660	64	540	54	66

4   24×12

A	B	C	D	E
288	48	306	36	28.8

Test 7 Answer Sheet

1   Ⓐ   Ⓑ   Ⓒ   Ⓓ   Ⓔ
2   Ⓐ   Ⓑ   Ⓒ   Ⓓ   Ⓔ
3   Ⓐ   Ⓑ   Ⓒ   Ⓓ   Ⓔ
4   Ⓐ   Ⓑ   Ⓒ   Ⓓ   Ⓔ

Test 8 Numerical Estimation

Now try another numerical estimation test. It also measures your ability to quickly estimate the answers to numerical calculations.

This type of test is often used in the selection of graduates and work-experienced personnel moving into applied technology areas. It can be used to select candidates for jobs such as electronics and electrical technicians, research technicians and many other technically orientated jobs.

Instructions: This test is a short one with only two questions. As in the previous test, you must *estimate* the answers, and then choose the answer which is nearest to your estimate from the 5 alternative answers. You will be discouraged from making precise calculations by a time constraint.

Indicate your answers by filling in completely the appropriate circles on the answer sheet. *Do not use a calculator.*

Time guideline: There is no official time guideline for this practice test. However, because in a real live test situation you will not be given sufficient time to calculate the exact answer, work as quickly as you possibly can.

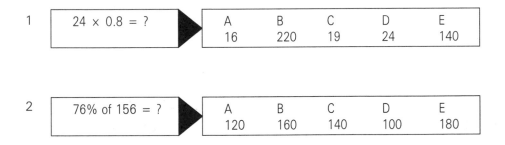

		A	B	C	D	E
1	$24 \times 0.8 = ?$	16	220	19	24	140
2	76% of 156 = ?	120	160	140	100	180

Test 8 Answer Sheet

	A	B	C	D	E
1	Ⓐ	Ⓑ	Ⓒ	Ⓓ	Ⓔ
2	Ⓐ	Ⓑ	Ⓒ	Ⓓ	Ⓔ

Test 9 Numerical Evaluation

This test measures your ability to evaluate or make deductions from complex numerical data laid out in the form of tables, graphs or charts. This type of test is often used in the selection and development of individuals over a wide range of sales or customer service roles.

Instructions: Look at the facts and figures presented in the various tables. In each question you are given five answers to choose from. One, and only one of the answers is correct in each case. Indicate your answer by filling in completely the appropriate circle on the answer sheet. *You may use a calculator.*

Time guideline: See how many questions you can answer in 5 minutes.

INTERNATIONAL PRODUCT SALES (Sales Revenue £ 000's)				
	Europe		North America	
Product Stock Codes	Last Year	This Year	Last Year	This Year
A002	17	31	410	354
B008	26	56	18	59
C015	21	69	27	71
D024	37	67	13	50
E001	31	32	19	37
F073	36	16	29	19

SOURCE OF COMPLAINTS TO TRAVEL AGENCY CUSTOMER SERVICES DEPARTMENT

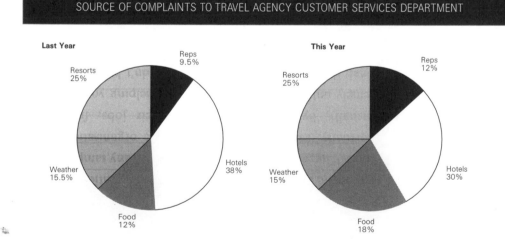

Last Year

Reps 9.5%
Resorts 25%
Weather 15.5%
Food 12%
Hotels 38%

This Year

Reps 12%
Resorts 25%
Weather 15%
Food 18%
Hotels 30%

1 Of the following, which had the highest sales revenue last year?

A	B	C	D	E
B008 in Europe	D024 in N America	E001 in Europe	C015 in N America	F073 in Europe

2 This year, which two sources together attracted more than half the complaints received?

A	B	C	D	E
Reps and Resorts	Food and Hotels	Hotels and Resorts	Resorts and Weather	Resorts and Food

3 If product E001 was sold at a price of £44.80 per unit this year, approximately how many units were sold in North America this year?

A	B	C	D	E
826	1,250	1,272	2,656	2,509

4 If last year, 'resorts' generated 600 complaints, how many complaints did 'hotels' generate?

A	B	C	D	E
900	912	930	945	968

5 If 'food' generated 330 complaints this year, representing an **increase** of 10% from last year, approximately how many complaints were there about 'weather' last year?

A	B	C	D	E
300	388	474	1833	2500

6 What was the approximate % increase in revenue generated by European sales of D024 from last year to this?

A	B	C	D	E
45%	55%	76%	81%	92%

Test 9 Answer Sheet

	A	B	C	D	E
1	Ⓐ	Ⓑ	Ⓒ	Ⓓ	Ⓔ
2	Ⓐ	Ⓑ	Ⓒ	Ⓓ	Ⓔ
3	Ⓐ	Ⓑ	Ⓒ	Ⓓ	Ⓔ
4	Ⓐ	Ⓑ	Ⓒ	Ⓓ	Ⓔ
5	Ⓐ	Ⓑ	Ⓒ	Ⓓ	Ⓔ
6	Ⓐ	Ⓑ	Ⓒ	Ⓓ	Ⓔ

Test 10 Interpreting Data

This test measures your ability to understand facts and figures in statistical tables and make logical deductions from the given information. Certainly, the ability to interpret data from a variety of different sources such as tables, graphs and charts is a common requirement in many managerial and professional jobs.

This type of test is often used to select candidates for administrative and supervisory jobs, as well as junior managers and management trainees, and any job involving analysis or decision-making based on numerical facts.

Instructions: For each question, indicate your answer by filling in completely the appropriate circle on the answer sheet. *Do not use a calculator. You may use rough paper for your workings-out.*

Time guideline: There is no official time guideline for this practice test, however, try to work through the questions as quickly as you can. Remember that accuracy is equally important.

Newspaper Readership				
	Readership (millions)		Percentage of Adults Reading each Paper in 1990	
Daily Newspapers	1981	1990	Males	Females
The Daily Chronicle	3.6	2.9	7	6
Daily News	13.8	9.3	24	18
The Tribune	1.1	1.4	4	3
The Herald	8.5	12.7	30	23
Daily Echo	4.8	4.9	10	12

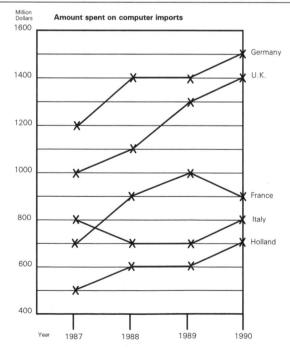

1   Which newsaper was read by a higher percentage of females than males in 1990?

A	B	C	D	E
The Tribune	The Herald	Daily News	Daily Echo	The Daily Chronicle

2   In 1989, how much more than Italy did Germany spend on computer imports?

A	B	C	D	E
650 million	700 million	750 million	800 million	850 million

3   What was the combined readership of the Daily Chronicle, Echo and Tribune in 1981?

A	B	C	D	E
10.6	8.4	9.5	12.2	7.8

4   If the amount spent on computer imports into the U.K. in 1991 was 20% lower than in 1990, what was spent in 1991?

A	B	C	D	E
1080	1120	1160	1220	1300

5   Which newspaper showed the largest change in female readership between 1981 and 1990?

A	B	C	D	E
Daily Echo	The Tribune	The Herald	The Daily Chronicle	Cannot Say

6   Which countries experienced a drop in the value of computers imported from one year to the next?

A	B	C	D	E
France & Italy	France & Holland	Holland & U.K.	U.K. & Italy	Italy & Holland

Test 10 Answer Sheet

	A	B	C	D	E
1	Ⓐ	Ⓑ	Ⓒ	Ⓓ	Ⓔ
2	Ⓐ	Ⓑ	Ⓒ	Ⓓ	Ⓔ
3	Ⓐ	Ⓑ	Ⓒ	Ⓓ	Ⓔ
4	Ⓐ	Ⓑ	Ⓒ	Ⓓ	Ⓔ
5	Ⓐ	Ⓑ	Ⓒ	Ⓓ	Ⓔ
6	Ⓐ	Ⓑ	Ⓒ	Ⓓ	Ⓔ

Test 11 Numerical Test

This test measures your ability to understand facts and figures in statistical tables and make logical deductions from the given information. The ability to interpret data from a variety of different sources such as tables, graphs and charts is a common requirement in many managerial and professional jobs.

This type of test is used in the selection of graduates, managers and supervisors over a wide range of industries.

Instructions: For each question you are given either five or ten options from which to choose. One, and only one of the answers is correct in each case. Indicate your answer by filling in completely the appropriate circle on the answer sheet. Please note that for questions which have 10 options you may have to fill in more than one circle to indicate your answer. *Some organisations allow the use of a calculator for this test, others do not. Therefore I suggest you try to manage without – at least to begin with.*

Time guideline: There is no official time guideline, however work as quickly as you can. *You may use rough paper for your workings-out.*

Statistical tables

Population Structure 1985

	Population at start of year (millions)	Live Births per 1000 population (Jan-Dec)	Deaths per 1000 population (Jan-Dec)	Percentage of population at start of year aged under 15	60 or over
UK	56.6	13.3	11.8	19	21
France	55.2	13.9	10.0	21	19
Italy	57.1	10.1	9.5	19	19
West Germany	61.0	9.6	11.5	15	20
Spain	38.6	12.1	7.7	23	17

Production of 15mm Buttons, July–December

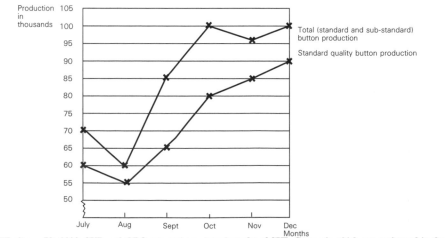

1   Which country had the highest number of people aged 60 or over at the start of 1985?

A	B	C	D	E
UK	France	Italy	W. Germany	Spain

2   What percentage of the total 15mm button production was classed as sub-standard in September?

A	B	C	D	E
10.5%	13%	15%	17.5%	20%
AB	AC	AD	AE	BC
23.5%	25%	27.5%	28%	30.5%

3   How many live births occurred in 1985 in Spain and Italy together (to the nearest 1000)?

A	B	C	D	E
104,000	840,000	1,044,000	8,400,000	10,440,000

4   What was the net effect on the UK population of the live birth and death rates in 1985?

A	B	C	D	E
Decrease of 66,700	Increase of 84,900	Increase of 85,270	Increase of 742,780	Cannot say

5   By how much did the total sales value of November's button production vary from October's?

A	B	C	D	E
£28.50 (Decrease)	£142.40 (Decrease)	£285.00 (Increase)	£427.50 (Decrease)	No change

6   What was the loss in potential sales revenue attributable to the production of sub-standard (as opposed to standard) buttons over the 6 month period?

A	B	C	D	E
£213.75	£427.50	£2,137.50	£2,280.00	£4,275.00

Test 11 Answer Sheet

	A	B	C	D	E
1	Ⓐ	Ⓑ	Ⓒ	Ⓓ	Ⓔ
2	Ⓐ	Ⓑ	Ⓒ	Ⓓ	Ⓔ
3	Ⓐ	Ⓑ	Ⓒ	Ⓓ	Ⓔ
4	Ⓐ	Ⓑ	Ⓒ	Ⓓ	Ⓔ
5	Ⓐ	Ⓑ	Ⓒ	Ⓓ	Ⓔ
6	Ⓐ	Ⓑ	Ⓒ	Ⓓ	Ⓔ

Answers to Numerical Reasoning questions

Test 6 Number Series

	A	B	C	D	E
1	Ⓐ	●	Ⓒ	Ⓓ	Ⓔ
2	Ⓐ	●	Ⓒ	Ⓓ	Ⓔ
3	Ⓐ	Ⓑ	●	Ⓓ	Ⓔ
4	Ⓐ	Ⓑ	●	Ⓓ	Ⓔ
5	●	Ⓑ	Ⓒ	Ⓓ	Ⓔ
6	Ⓐ	Ⓑ	Ⓒ	●	Ⓔ
7	●	Ⓑ	Ⓒ	Ⓓ	Ⓔ
8	●	Ⓑ	Ⓒ	Ⓓ	Ⓔ
9	Ⓐ	Ⓑ	●	Ⓓ	Ⓔ
10	●	Ⓑ	Ⓒ	Ⓓ	Ⓔ

Test 7 Numerical Estimation

	A	B	C	D	E
1	Ⓐ	Ⓑ	●	Ⓓ	Ⓔ
2	Ⓐ	●	Ⓒ	Ⓓ	Ⓔ
3	Ⓐ	Ⓑ	Ⓒ	●	Ⓔ
4	●	Ⓑ	Ⓒ	Ⓓ	Ⓔ

Test 8 Numerical Estimation

	A	B	C	D	E
1	Ⓐ	Ⓑ	●	Ⓓ	Ⓔ
2	●	Ⓑ	Ⓒ	Ⓓ	Ⓔ

Test 9 Numerical Evaluation

	A	B	C	D	E
1	Ⓐ	Ⓑ	Ⓒ	Ⓓ	●
2	Ⓐ	Ⓑ	●	Ⓓ	Ⓔ
3	●	Ⓑ	Ⓒ	Ⓓ	Ⓔ
4	Ⓐ	●	Ⓒ	Ⓓ	Ⓔ
5	Ⓐ	●	Ⓒ	Ⓓ	Ⓔ
6	Ⓐ	Ⓑ	Ⓒ	●	Ⓔ

Test 10 Interpreting Data

	A	B	C	D	E
1	Ⓐ	Ⓑ	Ⓒ	●	Ⓔ
2	Ⓐ	●	Ⓒ	Ⓓ	Ⓔ
3	Ⓐ	Ⓑ	●	Ⓓ	Ⓔ
4	Ⓐ	●	Ⓒ	Ⓓ	Ⓔ
5	Ⓐ	Ⓑ	Ⓒ	Ⓓ	●
6	●	Ⓑ	Ⓒ	Ⓓ	Ⓔ

Test 11 Numerical Test

	A	B	C	D	E
1	Ⓐ	Ⓑ	Ⓒ	●	Ⓔ
2	Ⓐ	Ⓑ	Ⓒ	●	Ⓔ
3	Ⓐ	Ⓑ	●	Ⓓ	Ⓔ
4	Ⓐ	●	Ⓒ	Ⓓ	Ⓔ
5	Ⓐ	Ⓑ	Ⓒ	Ⓓ	●
6	Ⓐ	Ⓑ	●	Ⓓ	Ⓔ

Numerical Reasoning Tests – How To Improve Your Performance

However numerical reasoning questions are presented, and at whatever level, you really do need a sound understanding of the following basic maths skills:

✓ addition
✓ subtraction
✓ multiplication
✓ division
✓ decimal numbers
✓ fractions
✓ percentages

This is essential, especially for questions which require any sort of mental calculation.

Remember that for many numerical reasoning tests, the use of a calculator is prohibited (however, take along a calculator, just in case).

Basic maths skills are all very well, but in higher level tests your ability to *reason* with numbers is also being tested. Here are some ways to improve your numerical reasoning ability:

◆ Practice maths with and without a calculator. Practising really does make a difference.
◆ Do number puzzles in newspapers and magazines.
◆ Keep score when playing games like darts, card games, etc.
◆ Calculate how much your shopping will cost before you reach the till.
◆ Work out how much change you should receive when you pay for something.
◆ Learn your times tables off by heart.
◆ Read financial reports in newspapers.
◆ Study tables of data.

CHAPTER EIGHT

Abstract Reasoning

Abstract reasoning tests, or diagrammatic reasoning tests as they are sometimes called, are psychometric tests which use diagrams, symbols, signs or shapes instead of words and numbers. In other words, they are *visual* questions. And because they require good visual-thinking skills rather than verbal or numerical skills, they are often considered to be a very good indicator of a person's general intellectual ability. For this reason they are given to applicants over a wide range of jobs.

All abstract reasoning tests are strictly timed, and *every single question will have one, and only one correct answer.*

In this chapter

In this chapter there are 4 different abstract reasoning tests for you to try. Before each one I've indicated for what sort of job, and for what industry, you might be expected to take that particular type of test.

At the end of this chapter there is section entitled **Abstract Reasoning Tests – How To Improve Your Performance** which is intended to help you do just that across the whole range of abstract reasoning tests. Included in this section are some hints on tackling the questions themselves. If you have a problem with any of the questions then hopefully the advice contained in this section will get you back on track. Remember, however, that all of us have strengths and weaknesses, and everyone will have some difficulty with some of the tests in this book.

Test 12 Diagrammatic Series

The following test measures your ability to recognise logical sequences within a series of diagrams or symbols.

This type of test is often used to assess reasoning skills at administrative, supervisory and junior management levels – in fact any occupation where logical or analytical reasoning is required. It could be used to select applicants for administrative and supervisory jobs, junior managers, management trainees, and jobs involving technical research or computer programming.

Instructions: Each problem in the test consists of a series of diagrams, on the left of the page, which follow a logical sequence. You are required to choose the next diagram in the series from the five options on the right. Indicate your answer by filling in completely the appropriate circle on the answer sheet.

Time guideline: See how many questions you can answer in 5 minutes. Remember to work accurately as well as quickly.

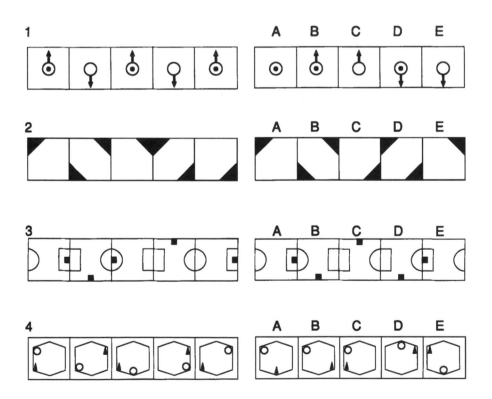

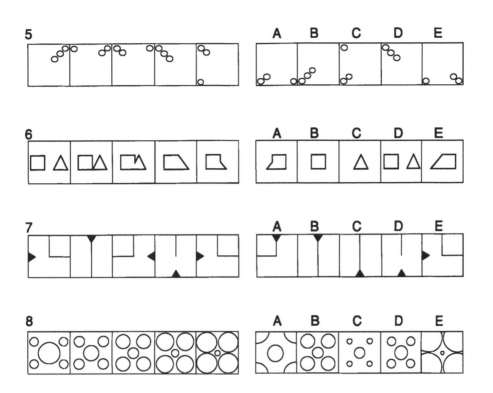

Test 12 Answer Sheet

	A	B	C	D	E
1	Ⓐ	Ⓑ	Ⓒ	Ⓓ	Ⓔ
2	Ⓐ	Ⓑ	Ⓒ	Ⓓ	Ⓔ
3	Ⓐ	Ⓑ	Ⓒ	Ⓓ	Ⓔ
4	Ⓐ	Ⓑ	Ⓒ	Ⓓ	Ⓔ
5	Ⓐ	Ⓑ	Ⓒ	Ⓓ	Ⓔ
6	Ⓐ	Ⓑ	Ⓒ	Ⓓ	Ⓔ
7	Ⓐ	Ⓑ	Ⓒ	Ⓓ	Ⓔ
8	Ⓐ	Ⓑ	Ⓒ	Ⓓ	Ⓔ

Test 13 Diagramming

This abstract reasoning test measures logical analysis through the ability to follow complex instructions. It simulates the ability to handle multiple and independent commands, an important ability in most IT jobs. This type of test is therefore specifically designed for the selection, development and promotion of staff working in the IT industry, for example, software engineers, systems analysts, programmers and database administrators.

Instructions: In this test, figures (shapes) in BOXES are presented in columns. They are changed in various ways by commands represented as symbols in CIRCLES. A complete list of these commands and what they do is shown below.

Time guideline: See how many questions you can answer in 4 minutes.

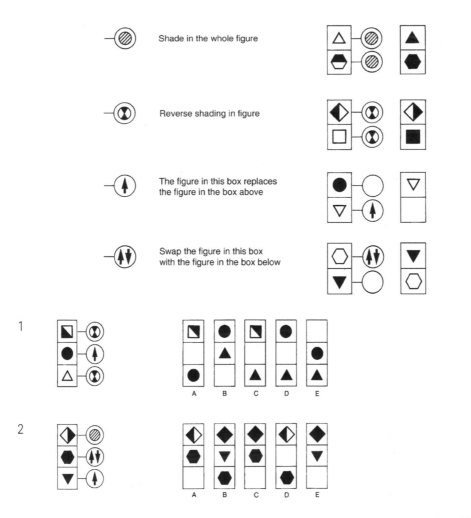

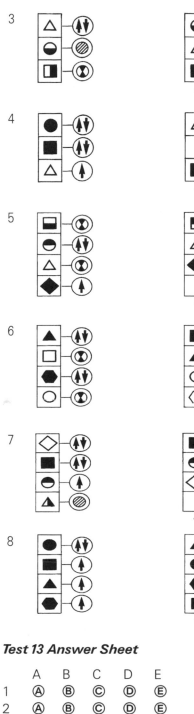

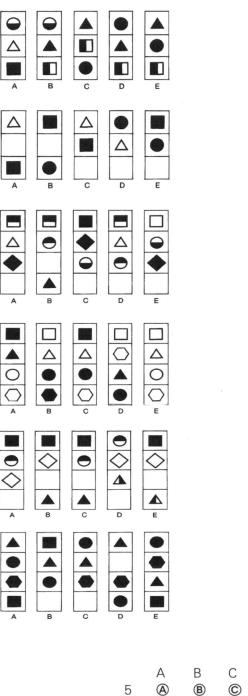

Test 13 Answer Sheet

	A	B	C	D	E			A	B	C	D	E
1	Ⓐ	Ⓑ	Ⓒ	Ⓓ	Ⓔ		5	Ⓐ	Ⓑ	Ⓒ	Ⓓ	Ⓔ
2	Ⓐ	Ⓑ	Ⓒ	Ⓓ	Ⓔ		6	Ⓐ	Ⓑ	Ⓒ	Ⓓ	Ⓔ
3	Ⓐ	Ⓑ	Ⓒ	Ⓓ	Ⓔ		7	Ⓐ	Ⓑ	Ⓒ	Ⓓ	Ⓔ
4	Ⓐ	Ⓑ	Ⓒ	Ⓓ	Ⓔ		8	Ⓐ	Ⓑ	Ⓒ	Ⓓ	Ⓔ

Test 14 Diagrammatic Reasoning

This abstract reasoning test measures your ability to infer a set of rules from a flow-chart, and apply these rules to new situations, and is specifically designed for the selection, development and promotion of staff working in the IT industry. It is a high-level measure of symbolic reasoning ability and is specially relevant in jobs that require the capacity to work through complex problems in a systematic and analytical manner, for example, in systems analysis and programming design.

Instructions: In this test you are shown a number of diagrams in which figures (shapes) in BOXES are altered by rules shown as symbols in CIRCLES. The rules can alter each figure by changing its colour, its size, its shape or by turning it upside down.

Paths through each diagram are shown as black or white arrows. You must follow paths which include only one type of arrow.

Work out what each rule does and then answer the questions below each diagram.

Time guideline: See how many questions you can answer in 4 minutes.

Look at the example below:

DIAGRAM

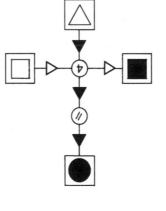

QUESTION

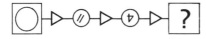

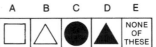

In the diagram, working horizontally, the white square becomes a black square so *ʏ* must be a colour changing rule. Working vertically, the white triangle becomes a black circle. Since we know that *ʏ* changes the colour of a figure, // must be a shape-changing rule. Applying these rules to the question, it is possible to identify that the white circle becomes a black triangle, so D is the correct answer to the question.

DIAGRAM

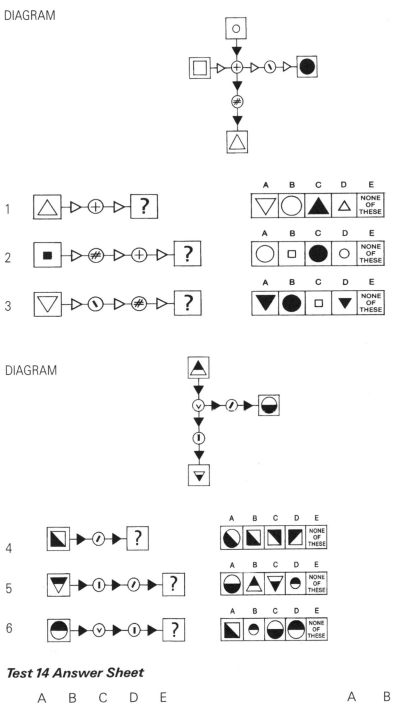

DIAGRAM

Test 14 Answer Sheet

	A	B	C	D	E			A	B	C	D	E
1	Ⓐ	Ⓑ	Ⓒ	Ⓓ	Ⓔ		4	Ⓐ	Ⓑ	Ⓒ	Ⓓ	Ⓔ
2	Ⓐ	Ⓑ	Ⓒ	Ⓓ	Ⓔ		5	Ⓐ	Ⓑ	Ⓒ	Ⓓ	Ⓔ
3	Ⓐ	Ⓑ	Ⓒ	Ⓓ	Ⓔ		6	Ⓐ	Ⓑ	Ⓒ	Ⓓ	Ⓔ

Test 15 Diagrammatic Thinking

The following test measures your ability to apply checks and follow a sequence of symbols arranged in a logical order. This type of test is often used in the selection of qualified school leavers for modern apprenticeship schemes and other technically orientated jobs.

It is also used to select graduates applying to work in applied technical areas, for example, electronics technicians, electrical technicians, research technicians and also for jobs tracking process control systems, debugging software and systems design.

Instructions: In this test you are required to follow the progress of a 'Development figure' which is changed according to instructions contained in a series of 'Process boxes'. These boxes are divided into three levels, each of which affects the development figure in a given way.

Time guideline: There is no official time guideline for this practice test, however, try to work through the questions as quickly as you can. Remember that accuracy is equally important as speed.

Process box		
Level 1	X	means change SHAPE from circle to square or vice versa
Level 2	X	means change SIZE from large to small or vice versa
Level 3	X	means change COLOUR from black to white or vice versa

NB: The absence of a cross means no change to that aspect of the figure.

Your task is to identify which process needs to be repeated at the end of the series in order to achieve the required 'Target' figure. Indicate your answer by fully blackening the appropriate circles A, B, C or D on Answer Sheet 19.

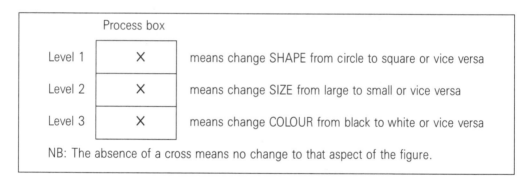

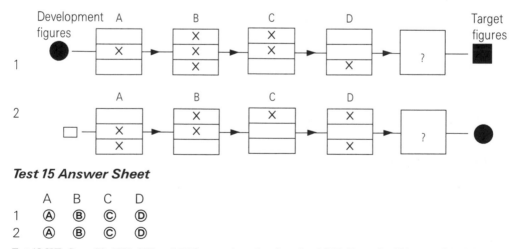

Test 15 Answer Sheet

	A	B	C	D
1	Ⓐ	Ⓑ	Ⓒ	Ⓓ
2	Ⓐ	Ⓑ	Ⓒ	Ⓓ

Answers to abstract reasoning questions

Test 12 – Diagrammatic Series

	A	B	C	D	E
1	Ⓐ	Ⓑ	Ⓒ	Ⓓ	●
2	Ⓐ	●	Ⓒ	Ⓓ	Ⓔ
3	Ⓐ	Ⓑ	Ⓒ	●	Ⓔ
4	Ⓐ	Ⓑ	Ⓒ	●	Ⓔ
5	Ⓐ	Ⓑ	●	Ⓓ	Ⓔ
6	Ⓐ	●	Ⓒ	Ⓓ	Ⓔ
7	Ⓐ	●	Ⓒ	Ⓓ	Ⓔ
8	Ⓐ	Ⓑ	Ⓒ	Ⓓ	●

Test 13 – Diagramming

	A	B	C	D	E
1	Ⓐ	Ⓑ	Ⓒ	●	Ⓔ
2	Ⓐ	Ⓑ	●	Ⓓ	Ⓔ
3	Ⓐ	●	Ⓒ	Ⓓ	Ⓔ
4	Ⓐ	Ⓑ	Ⓒ	Ⓓ	●
5	●	Ⓑ	Ⓒ	Ⓓ	Ⓔ
6	Ⓐ	Ⓑ	Ⓒ	Ⓓ	●
7	Ⓐ	●	Ⓒ	Ⓓ	Ⓔ
8	Ⓐ	Ⓑ	●	Ⓓ	Ⓔ

Test 14 – Diagrammatic Reasoning

	A	B	C	D	E
1	Ⓐ	●	Ⓒ	Ⓓ	Ⓔ
2	Ⓐ	Ⓑ	●	Ⓓ	Ⓔ
3	Ⓐ	Ⓑ	Ⓒ	●	Ⓔ
4	●	Ⓑ	Ⓒ	Ⓓ	Ⓔ
5	Ⓐ	Ⓑ	Ⓒ	●	Ⓔ
6	Ⓐ	Ⓑ	Ⓒ	Ⓓ	●

Test 15 – Diagrammatic Thinking

	A	B	C	D
1	Ⓐ	Ⓑ	●	Ⓓ
2	●	Ⓑ	Ⓒ	Ⓓ

Abstract Reasoning Tests – How To Improve Your Performance

◆ Try doing puzzles in newspapers, magazines and quiz books which involve diagrams.

◆ Play games which involve thinking out a problem visually and in a logical sequence, for example chess, Labyrinth, or computer Freecell.

◆ Abstract reasoning questions are often presented as sequences. Watch out for sequences which have separate components which work in different ways.

◆ At first glance, abstract reasoning questions may seem impossible. But by reading the instructions very carefully, and possibly by having a look at the answers to the first few questions, you'll see they are not so difficult after all.

CHAPTER NINE

Spatial Reasoning

There are people who may not be so hot with words or numbers, but are good with space. They can see an object in their mind, and manipulate it, turn it round, upside down, or pull it in and out of shape. These people are said to have good **spatial awareness**, and they often find success in the field of design, illustration, architecture, publishing, technology, electronic engineering and IT. Therefore it is hardly surprising to find employers in these industries using spatial reasoning tests to select applicants for jobs which require 3-dimensional perception.

The interesting thing about these test questions is that people with extremely good spatial awareness 'see' the solution immediately, without having to even think about it. But for most of us, the answers are not so obvious and you might need to make more of an effort to manipulate the shapes in your mind (or even do as I do – physically turn the page round).

In common with other psychometric tests, spatial reasoning tests are strictly timed, and *every single question has one, and only one correct answer.*

In this chapter

In this chapter there are 4 different spatial reasoning psychometric tests for you to try. Before each one I've indicated for what sort of job, or industry, you might be expected to take that particular type of test.

At the end of this chapter there is section entitled **Spatial Reasoning Tests – How To Improve Your Performance** which is intended to help you do just that. Included in this section are some hints on tackling the questions themselves. If you have a problem with any of the questions then hopefully the advice contained in this section will get you back on track. Remember, however, that all of us have strengths and weaknesses, and everyone will have some difficulty with some of the tests in this book.

Test 16 Spatial Recognition

The following test measures your ability to recognise shapes in two dimensions. This type of test is often used in the selection and development of personnel in technically or practically orientated jobs. The level is a little basic, however it is still used to assess graduates because of its technical content. You'll also find it a good warm up for the higher level Tests 18 and 19.

Instructions: In this test you are to choose the shape on the right which is identical to the given shape. The identical shape may be rotated on the page but not turned over. Indicate your answers by filling in completely the appropriate circles on the answer sheet.

Time guideline: See how many questions you can answer in 2 minutes. Remember to work accurately as well as quickly.

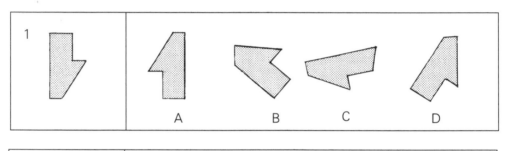

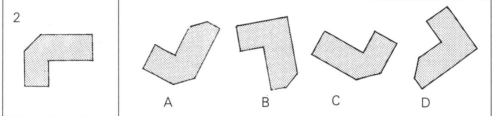

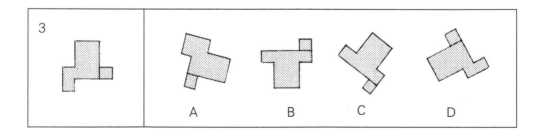

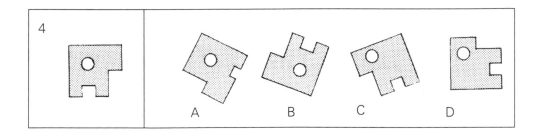

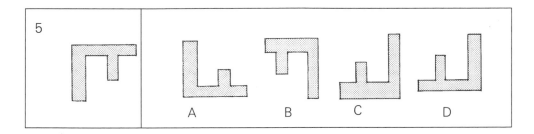

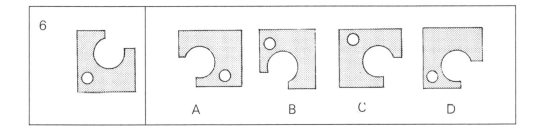

Test 16 Answer Sheet

	A	B	C	D
1	Ⓐ	Ⓑ	Ⓒ	Ⓓ
2	Ⓐ	Ⓑ	Ⓒ	Ⓓ
3	Ⓐ	Ⓑ	Ⓒ	Ⓓ
4	Ⓐ	Ⓑ	Ⓒ	Ⓓ
5	Ⓐ	Ⓑ	Ⓒ	Ⓓ
6	Ⓐ	Ⓑ	Ⓒ	Ⓓ

Test 17 Visual Estimation

The following test measures spatial perception and the ability to make accurate visual comparisons. This type of test is often used in the selection and development of personnel in technically or practically orientated jobs. As with the previous test, it's a good warm up for Tests 18 and 19.

Instructions: In this test you are to choose the two shapes which are identical and fill in the appropriate *two* circles on the answer sheet.

Time guideline: See how many questions you can answer in 2 minutes. Remember to work accurately as well as quickly.

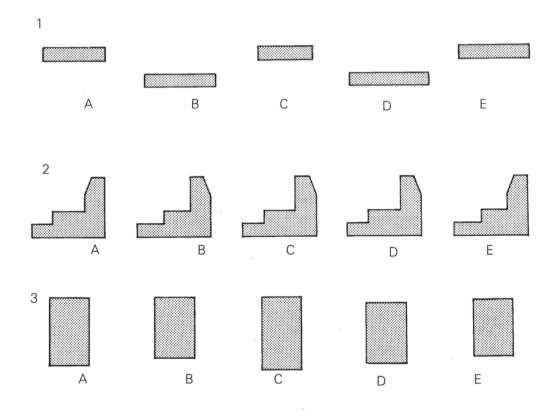

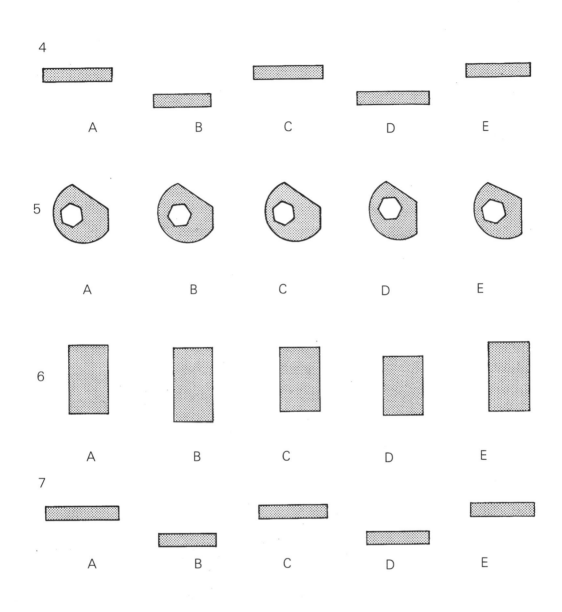

4

    A   B   C   D   E

5

    A   B   C   D   E

6

    A   B   C   D   E

7

    A   B   C   D   E

Test 17 Answer Sheet

	A	B	C	D	E
1	Ⓐ	Ⓑ	Ⓒ	Ⓓ	Ⓔ
2	Ⓐ	Ⓑ	Ⓒ	Ⓓ	Ⓔ
3	Ⓐ	Ⓑ	Ⓒ	Ⓓ	Ⓔ
4	Ⓐ	Ⓑ	Ⓒ	Ⓓ	Ⓔ
5	Ⓐ	Ⓑ	Ⓒ	Ⓓ	Ⓔ
6	Ⓐ	Ⓑ	Ⓒ	Ⓓ	Ⓔ
7	Ⓐ	Ⓑ	Ⓒ	Ⓓ	Ⓔ

Test 18 Spatial Reasoning

The following test measures your ability to visualise and manipulate shapes in three dimensions given a two-dimensional drawing. The test is high level, and could be used to select engineers, designers, draughtspeople and IT staff working with graphics or CAD/CAM software.

Instructions: In this test you are given a pattern which, if cut out, could be folded to make a three-dimensional shape (a box). You must decide which, if any, of the four boxes could be made by folding the pattern, and indicate this by filling in completely the appropriate circle on the answer sheet. If you think that none of the boxes could be made from the pattern, fill in circle 'E' on the answer sheet.

Time guideline: See how many questions you can answer in 3 minutes. Remember to work accurately as well as quickly.

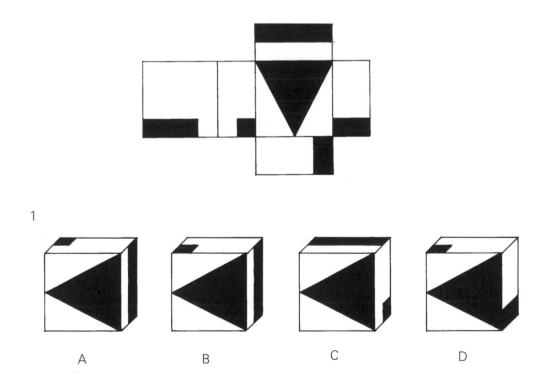

1

    A   B   C   D

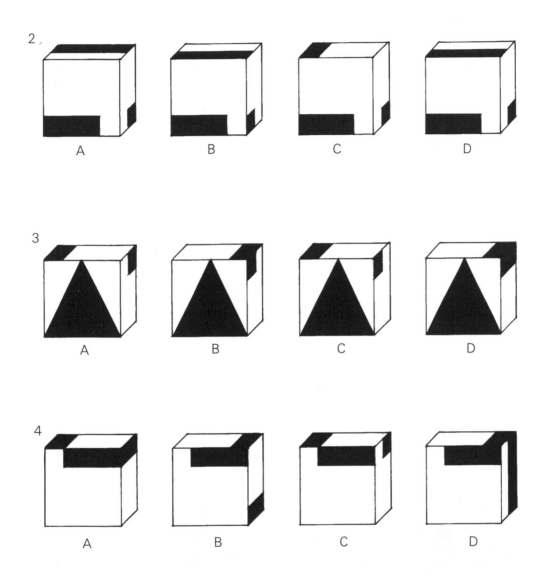

Test 18 Answer Sheet

	A	B	C	D	E
1	Ⓐ	Ⓑ	Ⓒ	Ⓓ	Ⓔ
2	Ⓐ	Ⓑ	Ⓒ	Ⓓ	Ⓔ
3	Ⓐ	Ⓑ	Ⓒ	Ⓓ	Ⓔ
4	Ⓐ	Ⓑ	Ⓒ	Ⓓ	Ⓔ

Test 19 Spatial Checking

This is another high level test, in this case measuring your ability to check designs and patterns. This type of test is used to select graduates in applied technology areas, for example, the design of electronic systems, engineering components and some applications of computer-aided design.

Time guideline: There is no official time guideline, just work as quickly and accurately as you can.

Instructions: In this test you are given a master layout with its own grid co-ordinates. To the right of this master layout are two copies, each of which differ from the master in one respect. Your task is to identify this difference and, using the co-ordinates shown on the master, indicate the grid reference by fully blackening the appropriate pair of circles on Answer Sheet 19. Note that copies are either rotated or flipped on the page.

MASTER

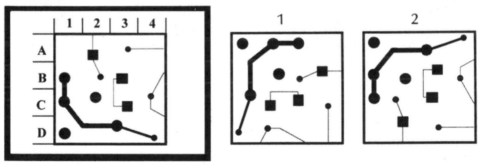

Test 19 Answer Sheet

1 ① ② ③ ④
  Ⓐ Ⓑ Ⓒ Ⓓ

2 ① ② ③ ④
  Ⓐ Ⓑ Ⓒ Ⓓ

Answers to spatial reasoning questions

Test 16 Spatial Recognition

	A	B	C	D
1	●	Ⓑ	Ⓒ	Ⓓ
2	Ⓐ	Ⓑ	●	Ⓓ
3	Ⓐ	Ⓑ	Ⓒ	●
4	Ⓐ	●	Ⓒ	Ⓓ
5	Ⓐ	Ⓑ	Ⓒ	●
6	Ⓐ	Ⓑ	●	Ⓓ

Test 17 Visual Estimation

	A	B	C	D	E
1	Ⓐ	●	Ⓒ	Ⓓ	●
2	Ⓐ	Ⓑ	●	●	Ⓔ
3	Ⓐ	●	Ⓒ	●	Ⓔ
4	●	Ⓑ	●	Ⓓ	Ⓔ
5	●	Ⓑ	●	Ⓓ	Ⓔ
6	●	Ⓑ	Ⓒ	Ⓓ	●
7	Ⓐ	Ⓑ	Ⓒ	●	●

Test 18 Spatial Reasoning

	A	B	C	D	E
1	Ⓐ	●	Ⓒ	Ⓓ	Ⓔ
2	Ⓐ	Ⓑ	Ⓒ	●	Ⓔ
3	Ⓐ	Ⓑ	●	Ⓓ	Ⓔ
4	Ⓐ	Ⓑ	Ⓒ	Ⓓ	●

Test 19 Spatial Checking

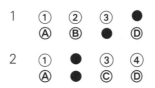

1	①	②	③	●
	Ⓐ	Ⓑ	●	Ⓓ
2	①	●	③	④
	Ⓐ	●	Ⓒ	Ⓓ

Spatial Reasoning Tests — How To Improve Your Performance

◆ Look at plans and DIY manuals.

◆ Do jigsaw puzzles and play chess.

◆ Assemble construction sets.

◆ Make up plans, patterns and designs.

◆ Make up simple patterns and try to visualise what they would look like when rotated or flipped over.

◆ Imagine how various objects look from different angles.

◆ Try to break down puzzles into chunks.

◆ Try drawing out the shapes in these tests on a sheet of paper. Actually handling the shapes and physically turning them round (or turning the book round) can help you understand how the 'puzzles' work.

◆ Try to get as much practice as you can.

If all else fails, look at the test questions and answers in this book at the same time. This should help you understand how spatial reasoning problems work.

CHAPTER TEN

Mechanical Comprehension

Mechanical comprehension tests are written, multiple-choice psychometric tests which are used as part of the selection procedure for technically or practically orientated jobs. They test your understanding of how mechanical and technical things work.

To a certain extent, you either have this ability or you don't. If you can answer the test questions in this chapter easily, you're probably a very practical person and always have been. If, on the other hand, you're like me and are incapable of even programming the DVD, it's unlikely that you'll be applying for a job in engineering or mechanics anyway.

But for those of you who enjoy taking your car to pieces and putting the bits back in the right places, I have included two mechanical comprehension tests for you to try.

As with other psychometric tests, mechanical comprehension tests are strictly timed, and *every single question will have one, and only one correct answer*.

In this chapter

In this chapter there are 2 mechanical comprehension tests. Before each test I have indicated for what sort of job, or what industry, you might be expected to take that particular type of test.

At the end of this chapter there is section entitled **Mechanical Comprehension Tests – How To Improve Your Performance** which is intended to help you do just that. Included in this section are some hints on tackling the questions themselves. If you have a problem with any of the questions then hopefully the advice contained in this section will get you back on track. Remember, however, that all of us have strengths and weaknesses, and everyone will have some difficulty with some of the tests in this book.

Test 20 Mechanical Comprehension

This test assesses your understanding of basic mechanical principles and their application to such devices as pulleys and gears and simple structures.

This type of test is often used in the selection and development of individuals in technically or practically orientated jobs, and in engineering and mechanics.

Instructions: Each problem in the test consists of a question which refers to a drawing. Choose the best answer to each question, indicating your answer by filling in completely the appropriate circle on the answer sheet.

Time guideline: There are 4 questions – see how many you can do in 2 minutes.

1   With which spanner will it be easier to undo the nut?

If equal, mark C.

2   Which shelf will support the heaviest load?

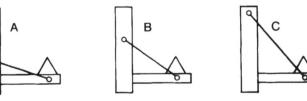

3   In which direction can pulley-wheel 'X' turn?

If it cannot turn, mark C.

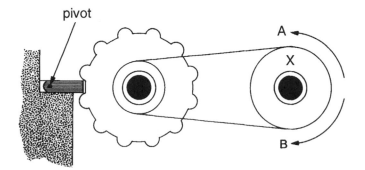

4   Which way will the pointer move when the shaft turns in the direction of the arrow?

If neither, mark C.

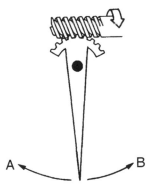

Test 20 Answer Sheet

	A	B	C
1	Ⓐ	Ⓑ	Ⓒ
2	Ⓐ	Ⓑ	Ⓒ
3	Ⓐ	Ⓑ	Ⓒ
4	Ⓐ	Ⓑ	Ⓒ

Test 21 Mechanical Comprehension

This test, which is more difficult than the previous one, also assesses your understanding of basic mechanical principles and their application to such devices as pulleys and gears and simple structures.

This type of test is often used in the selection and development of individuals in technically or practically orientated jobs. It is also used to recruit graduates or work experienced personnel moving into applied technology areas and jobs such as process control operators and electrical or research technicians, and in engineering and mechanics.

Instructions: The test is based on mechanical principles. Each problem in the test consists of a question which refers to a drawing. Choose the best answer to each question, indicating your answer by filling in completely the appropriate circle on the answer sheet.

Time guideline: There is no official time guideline for this practice test, however, try to work through the questions as quickly as you can.

1 Which screw is more likely to pull out of the wall when a load is applied to the hook?

   If equally likely, mark C.

2 Which apparatus requires less force to begin moving the block?

   If equal, mark C.

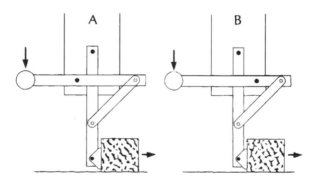

Test 21 Answer Sheet

	A	B	C
1	Ⓐ	Ⓑ	Ⓒ
2	Ⓐ	Ⓑ	Ⓒ

Answers to mechanical comprehension questions

Test 20 Mechanical Comprehension

	A	B	C
1	●	Ⓑ	Ⓒ
2	Ⓐ	Ⓑ	●
3	Ⓐ	●	Ⓒ
4	Ⓐ	●	Ⓒ

Test 21 Mechanical Comprehension

	A	B	C
1	●	Ⓑ	Ⓒ
2	Ⓐ	●	Ⓒ

Mechanical Comprehension Tests – How To Improve Your Performance

- Attempt lots of DIY.
- Try to understand how household objects work.
- Repair mechanical things, for example, a vacuum cleaner, a door lock.
- Take things to pieces and then reassemble them.
- Play with technical or construction sets.
- Build working models.

Looking at the answers to the questions should give you a better understanding of the underlying mechanical principles involved.

CHAPTER ELEVEN

Fault Diagnosis

Fault diagnosis tests are written, multiple-choice psychometric tests which are used as part of the selection procedure for technically or practically orientated jobs. They assess your ability to identify faults in logical systems – an important skill which has many applications including those of electronics fault finding, debugging of software, process control systems and systems design.

Skill in this area is all about the application of logical deduction, coupled with common sense, patience and curiosity.

As with other psychometric tests, fault diagnosis tests are strictly timed, and *every single question will have one, and only one correct answer.*

In this chapter

In this chapter there are 2 fault diagnosis practice tests for you to try. Before each test I have indicated for what sort of job, or for what industry, you might be expected to take that particular type of test.

At the end of this chapter there is section entitled **Fault Diagnosis Tests – How To Improve Your Performance** which is intended to help you do just that. However, remember that all of us have strengths and weaknesses, and everyone will have some difficulty with some of the tests in this book.

Test 22 Fault diagnosis

This test measures your ability to identify faults in systems. This type of test is often used in the selection of individuals in technically or practically orientated jobs such as skilled operatives, technical supervisors and jobs involving electronics fault finding. Although you might find it a little basic, it is still used to test graduates because of its technical content.

Time guideline: See how many questions you can answer in 3 minutes.

Instructions: You are required to follow sequences made up of a number of switches labelled A, B, C, and D. Each switch, when working properly, has a specified effect on a set of numbered lights (shown in a rectangle on the left). The rectangle on the right contains the result of that sequence.

In each case, **one** of the switches is not working and has no effect on the numbered lights. A list of the switches and what they can do is shown below.

Switch	Effect when working
A	Turns 1 and 2 on/off ie, black to white and vice versa
B	Turns 3 and 4 on/off ie, black to white and vice versa
C	Turns 1 and 3 on/off ie, black to white and vice versa
D	Turns 2 and 4 on/off ie, black to white and vice versa

○ = ON
● = OFF
Remember – a switch not working has no effect

Your task is to identify the switch which is not working in each sequence and indicate this by fully blackening the appropriate circle on Answer Sheet 22.

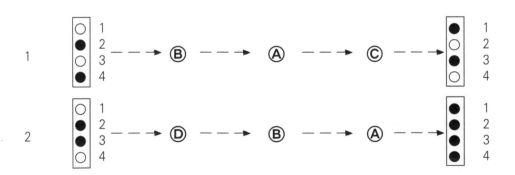

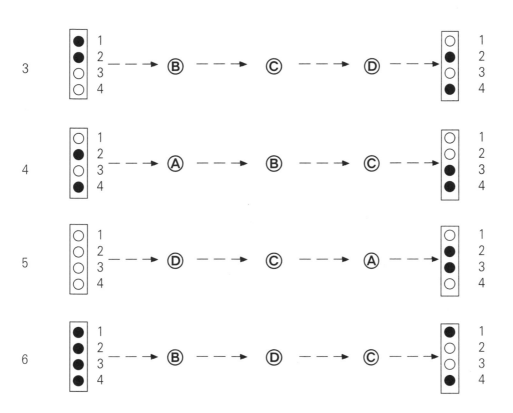

Test 22 Answer Sheet

	A	B	C	D
1	Ⓐ	Ⓑ	Ⓒ	Ⓓ
2	Ⓐ	Ⓑ	Ⓒ	Ⓓ
3	Ⓐ	Ⓑ	Ⓒ	Ⓓ
4	Ⓐ	Ⓑ	Ⓒ	Ⓓ
5	Ⓐ	Ⓑ	Ⓒ	Ⓓ
6	Ⓐ	Ⓑ	Ⓒ	Ⓓ

Test 23 Fault finding

This test measures your ability to identify faults in systems. This type of test is often used in the selection of graduates or work-experienced personnel moving into applied technology areas. Uses include electronics fault finding, debugging of software, process control systems and systems design.

Time guideline: There is no official time guideline for this test. However, try to work through the questions as quickly and as accurately as possible.

Instructions: You are required to follow sequences made up of a number of switches labelled A, B and C. Each switch, when working properly, has a specified effect on a set of numbered lights (shown in a square on the left). The circle on the right contains the result of a particular sequence.

In each case, **one** of the switches is not working and so has no effect on the numbered lights. A list of the switches and what they can do is shown below.

Switch	Effect when working
A	Turns 1 and 3 on/off i.e. from black to white or vice versa
B	Turns 3 and 4 on/off i.e. from black to white or vice versa
C	Turns 2 and 4 on/off i.e. from black to white or vice versa
	Remember – a switch that is not working has no effect

Your task is to identify the switch which is not working and indicate this by fully blackening the appopriate circles A, B or C on Answer Sheet 23.

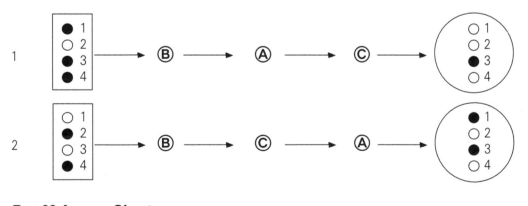

Test 23 Answer Sheet

	A	B	C
1	Ⓐ	Ⓑ	Ⓒ
2	Ⓐ	Ⓑ	Ⓒ

Answers to fault diagnosis questions

Test 22 Fault Diagnosis

	A	B	C	D
1	Ⓐ	Ⓑ	●	Ⓓ
2	Ⓐ	●	Ⓒ	Ⓓ
3	Ⓐ	Ⓑ	Ⓒ	●
4	Ⓐ	●	Ⓒ	Ⓓ
5	Ⓐ	Ⓑ	Ⓒ	●
6	Ⓐ	Ⓑ	●	Ⓓ

Test 23 Fault Finding

	A	B	C
1	Ⓐ	Ⓑ	●
2	Ⓐ	●	Ⓒ

Fault Diagnosis Tests – How To Improve Your Performance

◆ Think about the things that can go wrong with a piece of equipment, for example, a car, a washing machine, etc. What effect would any particular fault have? How would you diagnose the fault? What tests would pinpoint where the fault lay?

◆ Take an electronics course.

◆ Learn a programming language: HTML, Basic, C++, Java, and use it as much as possible.

For all these ideas there's simply no substitute for hands-on practical experience. At the beginning of this chapter I said that skill in this area is all about the application of logical deduction, coupled with common sense, patience and curiosity. If you already possess those qualities, practical experience is the thing which will most improve your performance.

CHAPTER TWELVE

Accuracy Tests

Tests that measure accuracy have various names. They can be called 'acuity tests', or 'clerical tests', but whatever the label they all basically do the same thing. They are multiple-choice tests which measure your ability to:

✓ deal with information
✓ follow instructions precisely
✓ work at high speed
✓ check material for errors
✓ maintain a high level of accuracy and concentration.

As with all the different types of psychometric test, tests of accuracy are strictly timed, and *every single question will have one, and only one correct answer.*

In this chapter

In this chapter there are 6 different tests for you to try. Before each one I've indicated for what sort of job, or what industry, you might be expected to take that particular type of test.

At the end of this chapter there is section entitled **Accuracy Tests – How To Improve Your Performance** which is intended to help you do just that. Included in this section are some hints on tackling the questions themselves. If you have a problem with any of the questions then hopefully the advice contained in this sections will get you back on track. However, remember that all of us have strengths and weaknesses, and everyone will have some difficulty with some of the tests in this book.

Test 24 Computer Checking

This test measures your ability to check input information with the corresponding output, ie, the accurate recording of new data onto a VDU screen or computer printout. The information may be re-ordered in some way, requiring both checking and scanning ability, as well as an element of simple reasoning.

This type of test is often used to select staff both at the clerical and supervisory level, in a variety of organisations including building societies, banks, retailers and many public sector organisations. Use it as a warm up for Tests 26, 27 and 28 which are more difficult.

Instructions: You are required to identify quickly and accurately whether the information has been correctly transferred to a VDU screen or computer printout. The output may be re-ordered in some way.

If there is an error in line 1 of the original document, fill in completely box A. If there is an error in line 2 of the original document, fill in completely box B. If there is an error in line 3 of the original document, fill in completely box C. If there is an error in line 4 of the original document, fill in completely box D. If there are no errors, fill in completely box E.

Time guideline: There is no official time guideline for this test. However, try to work through the questions as quickly and as accurately as possible.

1
★
★
★
★

Customer	582		
Invoice	X398		
Quantity	2	Size	36
Item	PD877	Value	18.99

2
★
★
★
★

Customer	379		
Invoice	X757		
Quantity	2	Size	10
Item	DX786	Value	9.50

3
★
★
★
★

Customer	323		
Invoice	Z819		
Quantity	3	Size	18
Item	ZX334	Value	36.90

4
★
★
★
★

Customer	414		
Invoice	B564		
Quantity	4	Size	18
Item	BT311	Value	31.99

114825 – 3			GENERAL COMMUNICATION AD5461		
RUN 4112			DATE 17 AUGUST		
INVOICE	CUSTOMER	QUANTITY	ITEM	SIZE	VALUE
X398	582	1	PD877	36	18.99
X757	397	2	DX786	12	9.50
Y213	664	1	LT468	40	25.00
Z819	323	3	ZX334	18	36.90
A742	443	5	BX021	2	12.50
B546	414	4	BT311	4	11.99
C611	452	1	BR121	6	2.49
C774	538	2	DX222	10	14.50
D775	543	1	BT223	11	15.00
D413	622	3	PT314	8	17.99
D276	422	6	ZD224	3	42.60
E119	123	3	LZ123	40	74.99
E772	232	1	DX223	10	14.22
E231	197	1	DX223	14	14.22
F332	772	1	BX223	4	15.00
F644	185	2	TD124	8	14.00
			END RUN 5421358 – 4		

Test 24 Answer Sheet

	A	B	C	D	E
1	Ⓐ	Ⓑ	Ⓒ	Ⓓ	Ⓔ
2	Ⓐ	Ⓑ	Ⓒ	Ⓓ	Ⓔ
3	Ⓐ	Ⓑ	Ⓒ	Ⓓ	Ⓔ
4	Ⓐ	Ⓑ	Ⓒ	Ⓓ	Ⓔ

Test 25 Coded Instructions

This test measures your ability to understand and follow written instructions when used in the form of coded language.

This type of test is often used to select staff both at the clerical and supervisory level, in a variety of organisations including building societies, banks, retailers and many public sector organisations. Use it as a warm up for Tests 26, 27 and 28 which are more difficult.

Instructions: The test consists of a series of passages containing instructions, each of which is followed by a number of questions. You are required to use the instructions in each passage to answer the questions which follow that passage. Indicate your answers each time by filling in completely the appropriate box A, B, C, D or E.

Time guideline: There is no official time guideline for this test. However, try to work through the questions as quickly and as accurately as possible.

Records Check

You are carrying out a computer check of personnel records.

If the staff member has left the organisation enter code L alone into the computer. For all staff members still present code P together with the appropriate check code below.

If the home address has changed enter code A: otherwise enter code B. If the home telephone number has changed enter code T. If the home telephone number is the same enter code C.

If the name of the staff member's doctor has changed enter code D: otherwise enter code N. If the doctor's telephone number has changed enter code R: if the telephone number is the same enter code S.

Code letters are to be entered in the sequence given above.

Which codes should be used to show the following records?

1 Employee number 1 is still a staff member. His address has changed but he has kept the same telephone number. There is no change to his doctor's details.

   A   P A N S

   B   A C N S

   C   P A C N S

   D   P A N C S

   E   P A C S N

2 Employee number 2 changed her doctor a year ago but in the past month has left the organisation.

A   L R

B   L N R

C   R L

D   L

E   L R N

3 Employee number 3 is still a staff member. His address and telephone number are the same and so is the name of his doctor. However, his doctor is operating from a different address and telephone number.

A   P B C R

B   P B C R N

C   P C N

D   L P B C R

E   P B C N R

4 Employee number 4 is still a staff member. Her address and telephone number are unchanged. Her doctor's name and telephone number are unchanged.

A   P B N

B   P B C N S

C   P N S B C

D   P A C N S

E   P B T N S

Test 25 Answer Sheet

	A	B	C	D	E
1	Ⓐ	Ⓑ	Ⓒ	Ⓓ	Ⓔ
2	Ⓐ	Ⓑ	Ⓒ	Ⓓ	Ⓔ
3	Ⓐ	Ⓑ	Ⓒ	Ⓓ	Ⓔ
4	Ⓐ	Ⓑ	Ⓒ	Ⓓ	Ⓔ

Test 26 Following Instructions

This test measures your ability to understand and follow written instructions. The topic covered is relevant to a technical environment although no prior knowledge of technical words is assumed.

This type of test is often used to select staff for modern apprenticeship schemes and other technically orientated jobs. It is also used to select graduates applying to work in applied technical areas, for example, electronics technicians, electrical technicians, research technicians.

Instructions: In this test you are given a written passage containing instructions. Use the instructions in the passage to answer the questions which follow. Indicate your answers each time by filling in completely the appropriate circle A, B, C or D.

Time guideline: There is no official time guideline for this test. However, try to work through the questions as quickly and as accurately as possible.

Photocopier Operation

Push the SORTER switch if the sorter is to be used to collate the copies (i.e. separate them into sets). The sort indicator is lit when this switch is on. If the lamp flashes, check the position of the sorter.

NO SORT mode   up to 99 copies can be made, all delivered to the top bin.

SORT mode   15 copies can be made from each original. The original can be up to 30 pages long. One copy of each original is delivered to each bin.

Originals should be arranged in reverse order when using the SORT mode.

---

1 What should you do if the sorter indicator flashes?

   A Push the SORTER switch.
   B Check the position of the sorter.
   C Disconnect the sorter.
   D Collate manually.

2 What is the maximum number of pages a document can have if the sorter is to be used?

   A 15.
   B 99.
   C 30.
   D No limit.

Test 26 Answer Sheet

	A	B	C	D
1	Ⓐ	Ⓑ	Ⓒ	Ⓓ
2	Ⓐ	Ⓑ	Ⓒ	Ⓓ

Test 27 Syntax Checking

This test measures your ability to check material quickly and accurately. These are important skills in any area of programming and especially important for computer data entry staff, software engineers, systems analysts, programmers and database administrators. This type of test is designed for applicants with graduate qualifications, or similar.

Instructions: In this test you will find lines taken from a mock programming language. Some lines do not conform to the rules of the language. Your task is to find which rules (if any) have been broken.

The rules for building these lines are found in the boxes below. There are two sorts of lines: those specified by an 'X' and those specified by a 'Y'. Each sort of line has its own set of 3 rules.

Using the appropriate set of rules, you must check which, if any, of the 3 rules have been broken. If a rule has been broken, fill in the appropriate circle on the answer sheet. More than one rule may be broken, so you may need to fill in more than one circle. If no rule has been broken, fill in circle D on the answer sheet.

Look at the following example:

X   Feature 16; update file list

This is an 'X' line, so look at the 'Rules for Building ''X'' lines'. Rule A has been broken, as there is no semi-colon at the end of the line. Rule B has been broken because the number 16 does not appear in brackets/parentheses. Therefore, circles A and B should be filled in, as below.

Example ● ● ⓒ ⒟

Time guideline: See how many of the following questions you can answer in 3 minutes.

Rules for Building 'X' lines	**Rules for Building 'Y' lines**
A Lines must end in a semi-colon	A Lines must begin with the word Comment
B Numbers must be in brackets/parantheses	B Numbers must be in quotation marks (ie ' ')
C All characters may be used except for # ' '	C All characters may be used except for . @ &

Remember, fill in circle D if no rules are broken.

Test 27 SHL Group Plc 2003. SHL and OPQ are registered trademarks of SHL Group plc which are registered in the United Kingdom and other countries.

1 X Set Var PQ to 10;

2 X Change character set to 'modern' Greek;

3 Y Comment Flag next 5 lines.

4 Y Comment. Move (file) To Directory (new)

5 Y Comment Read Value From Register (2);

6 X Stop run if ABC < (23);

7 Y Copy All Strings equal to '6' & '7' letters to buffer '1'

8 Y Comment Let String – '10'

9 X Allocate Demarcation (#) Bounds

10 Y If A Greater Than 10, Replace Value A With Upper Value B

11 X Enable's Automatic Printing, Speed # 200;

12 X Cut file (XY) from line (8) to line 921);

Test 27 Answer Sheet

	A	B	C	D			A	B	C	D
1	Ⓐ	Ⓑ	Ⓒ	Ⓓ		7	Ⓐ	Ⓑ	Ⓒ	Ⓓ
2	Ⓐ	Ⓑ	Ⓒ	Ⓓ		8	Ⓐ	Ⓑ	Ⓒ	Ⓓ
3	Ⓐ	Ⓑ	Ⓒ	Ⓓ		9	Ⓐ	Ⓑ	Ⓒ	Ⓓ
4	Ⓐ	Ⓑ	Ⓒ	Ⓓ		10	Ⓐ	Ⓑ	Ⓒ	Ⓓ
5	Ⓐ	Ⓑ	Ⓒ	Ⓓ		11	Ⓐ	Ⓑ	Ⓒ	Ⓓ
6	Ⓐ	Ⓑ	Ⓒ	Ⓓ		12	Ⓐ	Ⓑ	Ⓒ	Ⓓ

Test 28 Computer Checking

This test measures speed and accuracy in the checking of character strings made up of letters, numbers and symbols. These are important skills in any area of programming and especially important for computer data entry staff, software engineers, systems analysts, programmers and database administrators. This type of test is designed for applicants with graduate qualifications, or similar.

Instructions: Find the two sets of characters which are the same in each line and mark the letters for the two appropriate columns (A, B, C, D or E) on the answer section.

Time guideline: There are 20 questions – see how many you can do in 3 minutes.

	A	B	C	D	E
1	15*TZ	1*5TZ	15*T2	15*TZ	IS*TZ
2	TVB$	TBV$	TBVS	TB$V	TBV$
3	GS24B	G2S4B	GS24B	GS2B4	GS42B
4	LOGGB	LO6GB	LOGG8	LOG68	LOG68
5	$*T(	$*T(	$*2(	S*2(	$*T)
6	986538	968538	986588	968538	998538
7	B27JP	B2J7P	B277P	B27PP	B277P
8	PC4#!	PC7#!	PC47!	PC4#1	PC4#!
9	GA!9%	GA!98	GA198	GA!98	GA19%
10	D*8XD	D*X*D	DX8XD	DX8XD	D*86D

11	969G)	669G)	696G)	669G)	669G)
12	EO(((()	EO((()	EO(())	EO(())	EO()))
13	HEX09	HEX07	#EX09	H4X0P	HEX09
14	47S$	44S$$	47S$$	44SS$	44S$$
15	NVBR	NVR8	NVRB	NVRB	NVBB
16	69LBJ	69BLJ	99LBJ	69LBJ	69LJB
17	TXENE	TTENE	TXENN	TEXNE	TXENE
18	08%%Q	088%Q	0%8%Q	Q8%%Q	088%Q
19	LOP23	LOB23	LOP32	LOB32	LOB23
20	A79QA	A7Q9A	A790A	A970A	A970A

Test 28 Answer Sheet

	A	B	C	D	E
1	Ⓐ	Ⓑ	Ⓒ	Ⓓ	Ⓔ
2	Ⓐ	Ⓑ	Ⓒ	Ⓓ	Ⓔ
3	Ⓐ	Ⓑ	Ⓒ	Ⓓ	Ⓔ
4	Ⓐ	Ⓑ	Ⓒ	Ⓓ	Ⓔ
5	Ⓐ	Ⓑ	Ⓒ	Ⓓ	Ⓔ
6	Ⓐ	Ⓑ	Ⓒ	Ⓓ	Ⓔ
7	Ⓐ	Ⓑ	Ⓒ	Ⓓ	Ⓔ
8	Ⓐ	Ⓑ	Ⓒ	Ⓓ	Ⓔ
9	Ⓐ	Ⓑ	Ⓒ	Ⓓ	Ⓔ
10	Ⓐ	Ⓑ	Ⓒ	Ⓓ	Ⓔ
11	Ⓐ	Ⓑ	Ⓒ	Ⓓ	Ⓔ
12	Ⓐ	Ⓑ	Ⓒ	Ⓓ	Ⓔ
13	Ⓐ	Ⓑ	Ⓒ	Ⓓ	Ⓔ
14	Ⓐ	Ⓑ	Ⓒ	Ⓓ	Ⓔ
15	Ⓐ	Ⓑ	Ⓒ	Ⓓ	Ⓔ
16	Ⓐ	Ⓑ	Ⓒ	Ⓓ	Ⓔ
17	Ⓐ	Ⓑ	Ⓒ	Ⓓ	Ⓔ
18	Ⓐ	Ⓑ	Ⓒ	Ⓓ	Ⓔ
19	Ⓐ	Ⓑ	Ⓒ	Ⓓ	Ⓔ
20	Ⓐ	Ⓑ	Ⓒ	Ⓓ	Ⓔ

Answers to Accuracy Tests

Test 24 Computer Checking

	A	B	C	D	E
1	Ⓐ	Ⓑ	●	Ⓓ	Ⓔ
2	●	Ⓑ	●	Ⓓ	Ⓔ
3	Ⓐ	Ⓑ	Ⓒ	Ⓓ	●
4	Ⓐ	●	●	●	Ⓔ

Test 25 Coded Instructions

	A	B	C	D	E
1	Ⓐ	Ⓑ	●	Ⓓ	Ⓔ
2	Ⓐ	Ⓑ	Ⓒ	●	Ⓔ
3	Ⓐ	Ⓑ	Ⓒ	Ⓓ	●
4	Ⓐ	●	Ⓒ	Ⓓ	Ⓔ

Test 26 Following Instructions

	A	B	C	D
1	Ⓐ	●	Ⓒ	Ⓓ
2	Ⓐ	Ⓑ	●	Ⓓ

Test 27 Syntax Checking

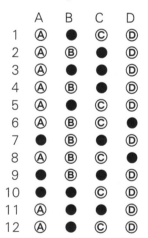

	A	B	C	D
1	Ⓐ	●	Ⓒ	Ⓓ
2	Ⓐ	Ⓑ	●	Ⓓ
3	Ⓐ	●	●	Ⓓ
4	Ⓐ	Ⓑ	●	Ⓓ
5	Ⓐ	●	Ⓒ	Ⓓ
6	Ⓐ	Ⓑ	Ⓒ	●
7	●	Ⓑ	●	Ⓓ
8	Ⓐ	Ⓑ	Ⓒ	●
9	●	Ⓑ	●	Ⓓ
10	●	●	Ⓒ	Ⓓ
11	Ⓐ	●	●	Ⓓ
12	Ⓐ	●	Ⓒ	Ⓓ

Test 28 Computer Checking

	A	B	C	D	E
1	●	Ⓑ	Ⓒ	●	Ⓔ
2	Ⓐ	●	Ⓒ	Ⓓ	●
3	●	Ⓑ	●	Ⓓ	Ⓔ
4	Ⓐ	Ⓑ	Ⓒ	●	●
5	●	●	Ⓒ	Ⓓ	Ⓔ
6	Ⓐ	●	Ⓒ	●	Ⓔ
7	Ⓐ	Ⓑ	●	Ⓓ	●
8	●	Ⓑ	Ⓒ	Ⓓ	●
9	Ⓐ	●	Ⓒ	●	Ⓔ
10	Ⓐ	Ⓑ	●	●	Ⓔ
11	Ⓐ	●	Ⓒ	●	Ⓔ
12	Ⓐ	Ⓑ	●	●	Ⓔ
13	●	Ⓑ	Ⓒ	Ⓓ	●
14	Ⓐ	●	Ⓒ	Ⓓ	●
15	Ⓐ	Ⓑ	●	●	Ⓔ
16	●	Ⓑ	Ⓒ	●	Ⓔ
17	●	Ⓑ	Ⓒ	Ⓓ	●
18	Ⓐ	●	Ⓒ	Ⓓ	●
19	Ⓐ	●	Ⓒ	Ⓓ	●
20	Ⓐ	Ⓑ	Ⓒ	●	●

Accuracy Tests – How To Improve Your Performance

◆ Use catalogues and timetables.

◆ Check the football or financial results.

◆ Play games involving checking numbers and letters.

◆ Read lots of instructions for using things, for example, a digital clock or video recorder.

◆ Read lots of instructions for making or repairing things, for example, a cake, fixing a fuse, and check that you understand what you're reading.

◆ Try looking at manuals and instructions for games, appliances and computers.

Accuracy tests demand a very high level of concentration, so treat yourself to a short break every now and then. Sit up straight, shut your eyes and take a few deep breaths, just for 20 seconds or so. This will help you stay alert, relax you a little, and give your eyes and brain a well deserved rest.

CHAPTER THIRTEEN

Combination Tests

So far, all the psychometric tests in this book have been very specific; each one of them measuring a certain ability, be it verbal, numerical, mechanical and so on.

However, out there in the big wide world, there are employers who do not use accredited and well researched psychometric tests from well established test publishers like SHL – they make up their own tests themselves. I have decided to include one of these tests.

It's what I call a *combination* test because it is a mixture of verbal reasoning, number problems and abstract puzzles, with one or two spatial reasoning questions thrown in for good measure. The company that uses it recruits graduates of the highest calibre into software engineering jobs.

Now, you might be thinking, 'How can a test like this sort out potentially good software engineers from bad ones? How is knowing in which month of the year the 47th week appears relevant to the skills needed by the IT industry?'

The answer is surprising – there isn't really any relevance at all! The company who uses this test isn't trying to measure verbal ability, nor numerical ability, nor general knowledge. What they are interested in is **speed of thought**. They want people who can think quickly.

Speed of thought is an essential attribute for a software engineer. In a commercial world, projects completed quickly mean larger profits and an enhanced reputation for the company in question.

And there's another reason I've included this test – it's quite good fun!

Test 29 Combination Test

Instructions: The objective of the test is to answer correctly as many questions as possible in 12 minutes. Simply tick the letter corresponding to your answer underneath each question.

Although many of the questions are not particularly difficult, you'll need all the concentration you can muster to beat the clock, so sit somewhere quiet where you won't be disturbed.

Time guide: There are 44 questions. See how many you can do in 12 minutes.
The answers are at the end of the chapter.

1   The 47th week of the year is in:

(a)   December
(b)   November
(c)   September
(d)   June
(e)   January

2   Does IQ stand for Intellectual Quotient?

(a)   Yes
(b)   No

3   Which word is different from the rest?

(a)   whimsical
(b)   playful
(c)   capricious
(d)   uncanny
(e)   comical

4   Pick the number that follows the pattern set by the series:

0   1   3   6   10 __

(a)   6
(b)   14
(c)   15
(d)   16

5   Which one of these forms does not belong with the rest?

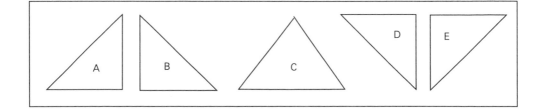

6 STRANGE is the opposite of:

  (a) similar
  (b) familiar
  (c) peculiar
  (d) obstinate
  (e) happy

7 One orange cost 12 pence. A dozen and a half oranges will cost:

  (a) £1.44
  (b) £2.16
  (c) £0.30
  (d) £1.80
  (e) £2.06

8 HARSH is the opposite of:

  (a) stern
  (b) mild
  (c) severe
  (d) warm
  (e) weather

9 OBVIOUS is the opposite of:

  (a) apparent
  (b) clear
  (c) obscure
  (d) visible
  (e) conspicuous

10 Which of the following numbers does not fit in with the pattern of this series?

  64 54 42 31 20

  (a) 64
  (b) 54
  (c) 42
  (d) 31
  (e) 20

11 Which one of these forms does not belong with the rest?

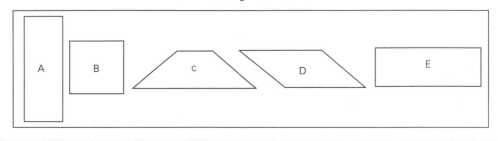

12 If most Gannucks are Dorks and most Gannucks are Xorgs, the statement that some Dorks are Xorgs is:

(a) True
(b) False
(c) Indeterminable from data

13 A car dealer spent £20,000 for some used cars. He sold them for £27,500 making an average of £1,500 on each car. How many cars did he sell?

(a) 4
(b) 11
(e) 5
(d) 15
(e) 7

14 What is the opposite of ABDICATE?

(a) occupy
(b) edit
(c) court
(d) attempt
(e) abandon

15 If you put the following words into a meaningful statement, what would the last word be?

(a) fall
(b) a
(c) before
(d) pride
(e) comes

16 Which of the following words is related to SOUND as FOOD is to MOUTH?

(a) ear
(b) stomach
(c) music
(d) orchestra
(e) throat

17 Tom and Harry caught a dozen fish. Harry caught twice as many as Tom. How many did Tom catch?

(a) 2
(b) 4
(c) 8
(d) 6
(e) 3

18   Which of the following numbers doesn't fit the sequence?

13   18   14   19   15   21   16

(a)   13
(b)   18
(c)   14
(d)   19
(e)   15
(f)   21
(g)   16

19   Which letter does not belong in the sequence?

C   F   J   M   Q   U

(a)   C
(b)   F
(c)   J
(d)   M
(e)   Q
(f)   U

20   If George met Gertrude and Gertrude met Ralph, then the statement that George and Ralph did not meet is:

(a)   True
(b)   False
(c)   Indeterminable

21   If it takes four bricklayers an hour to build a wall, how long will it take five of them to build the same wall?

(a)   90 minutes
(b)   45 minutes
(c)   50 minutes
(d)   48 minutes
(e)   40 minutes

22   What is the opposite of REPUDIATE?

(a)   encourage
(b)   crime
(c)   endorse
(d)   disappoint
(e)   halt

23   The first four forms are alike in a certain way. Pick the numbered form that is also alike:

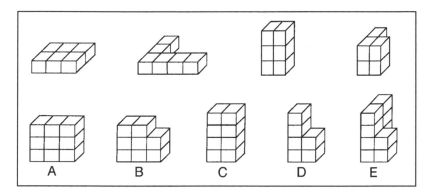

24   If Bob is older than Harry and Harry is older than Sue, the statement that Sue is younger than Bob is:

(a)   True
(b)   False
(c)   Indeterminable from data

25   What is the opposite of IMBUE?

(a)   prize
(b)   tasteful
(c)   texture
(d)   invest
(e)   clear

26   A bag of coffee beans costs £30 and contains 100 possible servings. However, typical wastate averages 25%. For how much must the proprietor sell a cup of coffee to make a 150% profit per bag?

(a)   £1.25
(b)   £0.75
(c)   £1.00
(d)   £2.00
(e)   none of these answers are right

27   If a pair of trousers takes one-and-a-half as much cloth as a shirt, and the total cloth used for the trousers and the shirt is £50, how much does the cloth for the trousers cost?

(a)   £25
(b)   £20
(c)   £30
(d)   £40
(e)   none of these answers

28   Complete the comparison: BOOK is to LIBRARY as PAINTING is to

    (a)   artists
    (b)   curator
    (c)   easel
    (d)   gallery
    (e)   building

29   What meaning do the following two statements have?

Don't put all your eggs in one basket.
Don't count your chickens before they hatch.

    (a)   same
    (b)   opposite
    (c)   neither the same nor opposite

30   Which one of the following numbers doesn't fit the pattern?

5/8 9/24 1/4 2/16 0

    (a)   5/8
    (b)   9/24
    (c)   1/4
    (d)   2/16
    (e)   0

31   Complete the comparison: BISHOP is to CHESS as SOLDIER is to

    (a)   battlefield
    (b)   war
    (c)   government
    (d)   army
    (e)   gun

32   Pick the piece that's missing from the puzzle.

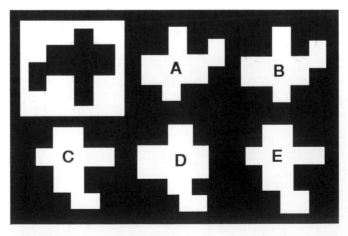

33 The following statements:

Hindsight is always 20/20
Can't see the trees for the forest

(a)   are the same in meaning
(b)   are opposite in meaning
(c)   are neither the same nor oppsite in meaning

34 A zoo has some lions and some ostriches. The zoo keeper counted 15 heads and 50 legs. How
many lions were there?

(a)   9
(b)   10
(c)   11
(d)   12
(e)   13
(f)   14

35 A sushi restaurant buys twenty fish for £10 each. The owner knows that 50% of the fish will go
bad before being served. Each fish creates 10 servings. What price must they charge per serving
in order to make a 100% profit on their initial investment?

(a)   £4
(b)   £2
(c)   £3
(d)   £6
(e)   £20

36 The words SURREPTITIOUS and SUSPICIOUS mean:

(a)   same
(b)   opposite
(c)   neither the same nor opposite

37 Three partners venture on a project. They pro-rate their (potential) profits over their £11,000
investment. Dan invests twice as much as Pete. Pete invests 50% more than Phil. If the venture
breaks even how much does Phil get back?

(a)   £6000
(b)   £2500
(c)   £2000
(d)   £3666.66
(e)   0

38   A basketball player shoots 33% from the foul line. How many shots must he take to make 100 baskets?

(a)   300
(b)   301
(c)   304
(d)   100
(e)   333

39   All Nerds are Jerks and some Nerds are Geeks. A few Geeks are BrainMasters, therefore all Brainmasters are Jerks.

(a)   True
(b)   False
(c)   Indeterminable from data

40   A submarine averages 10 miles an hour under water and 25 miles per hour on the surface. How many hours will it take it to make a 350 mile trip if it goes two-and-a-half times further on the surface?

(a)   10
(b)   15
(c)   35
(d)   20
(e)   65

41   A man was given eight pound coins. However, one of them was fake and he did not know if the fake coin weighed more or less than the other coins. What is the minimum number of weighings that it would take to guarantee him finding the counterfeit coin? Assume a balance scale is used.

(a)   2
(b)   3
(c)   7
(d)   12
(e)   Indeterminable from data

42   Which number does not fit within the following sequence?

1/5 1/6   1/8   1/10   1/15   1/30

(a)   1/5
(b)   1/6
(c)   1/8
(d)   1/10
(e)   1/15
(f)   1/30

43   At the end of a banquet 10 people shake hands with each other. How many handshakes will there be in total?

  (a)   100
  (b)   90
  (c)   45
  (d)   20
  (e)   50

44   Complete the comparison: SOLICITOR is to ADVISER as SYCOPHANT is to:

  (a)   ruffian
  (b)   fawner
  (c)   nobleman
  (d)   blackmailer
  (e)   flautist

Answers to combination test

Now here are the answers. For your information, the company who uses this test considers a score of 30 or more *correct* answers good enough to move a candidate on to the next stage in the recruitment process. No one has ever scored full marks.

1	b	23	d
2	b	24	a
3	d	25	e
4	c	26	c
5	c	27	c
6	b	28	d
7	b	29	c
8	b	30	a
9	c	31	b
10	b	32	c
11	c	33	c
12	a	34	b
13	c	35	a
14	a	36	c
15	a	37	c
16	a	38	c
17	b	39	c
18	f	40	d
19	f	41	b
20	c	42	c
21	d	43	c
22	c	44	b

CHAPTER FOURTEEN

Personality Questionnaires

Personality questionnaires are psychometric tests which assess the different aspects of personality, character, and behaviour relevant to the world of work.

However, personality questionnaires, or 'self-reports' as they are sometimes called, are not tests in the true sense of the word, for two reasons:

1. there are no right or wrong answers
2. they are not timed.

What they are, though, is popular. Written by occupational psychologists and administered by trained HR personnel, their use has increased dramatically in the last few years. From shelf-stacker to director, apply for a job with any medium to large organisation, commercial or otherwise, and I can virtually guarantee you will be asked to complete a personality questionnaire.

The results of the personality questionnaire could determine your overall suitability to work for a particular organisation, or place you in an appropriate department or team once the decision has already been made to employ you. They're also very useful for recruiters, because it gives them something to talk about when they interview you.

There are **two** main types of personality questionnaire. The first is often referred to in HR jargon as 'competency' questionnaires.

Competency questionnaires

Competency questionnaires tend to be pretty short, and they focus on behavioural actions, which are things like:

◆ Managerial qualities (leadership, planning, organisation, attention to detail and persuasiveness).

◆ Professional qualities (specialist knowledge, problem solving, analytical ability, oral and written communication).

◆ Entrepreneurial qualities (commercial awareness, creativity, understanding of the need to plan for the longer term).

◆ Personal qualities (an ability to work well with other people, flexibility, resilience and motivation).

Competency questionnaires are frequently used on application forms and online application forms. Here's an example of the sort of question you might get:

I am the sort of person who....

1. A Easily establishes rapport with reports.
   B Influences the course of meetings.
   C Speaks coherently.
   D Encourages colleagues to meet objectives.

2. A Writes creatively.
   B Seeks answers to problems.
   C Is effective in communicating requirements.
   D Is aware of costs.

For each question you have to decide which statement is the most like you and also which is the least like you – not an easy task.

   Competency-type questions are also a favourite with interviewers who, analysing the answers you gave on the application form test, like to hit graduates with questions like:

'*Tell me about a situation in which planning and organisation was vitally important to you.*'

You can see what they're getting at; they want to know how you behave in the work situation. If, as a student, you have no formal work experience, think about how you behaved in similar situation at university, or another time in your life.

The way competency questionnaires are scored is that generally, each organisation using them chooses a small number of qualities which they feel are essential to the particular job, and use these to put together their own unique scoring key. Very sensible actually, since nobody in the world has all the qualities listed above.

So if you are rejected by a company on the basis of an application form test, don't worry. You could possibly be the 'wrong' sort of person for them, but perfect for the next company you apply to. Therefore I'd say it's best to forget about the scoring mechanism and just answer as honestly as you can, because it's in your interest to do so.

True personality questionnaires

True personality questionnaires are usually much longer than competency-type questionnaires. For example, one version of SHL's very well known *OPQ* 32, which asks you to answer questions in a similar format to the Rating Statements test shown below, has 230 items. Another version, which is similar to the Making Choices test, also shown below, has 104 blocks.

Personality questionnaires are generally used when you go along to be interviewed, or when you attend an assessment centre. They are scored by measuring the test result against 32 different dimensions of personality. These include:

◆ Relationships with people (how persuasive, controlling, outgoing, modest, caring, democratic, independently minded, confident or outspoken you are).

◆ Your thinking style (how rational, evaluative, conventional, conceptual, innovative, forward thinking, detail conscious, conscientious or rule-following you are).

◆ Your feelings and emotions (how relaxed, worrying, tough-minded, optimistic, trusting, emotionally controlled, vigorous, competitive, achieving or decisive you are).

Personality questionnaires measuring these qualities are used extensively to select graduates, but if the list looks a little daunting, don't worry. As with competency questionnaires, companies are just looking for the 'right' people – which means you could turn out to be the 'wrong' sort of person for one, but perfect for another.

How can personality questionnaires be valid when candidates rate their own behaviours?

Recruiting organisations are fully aware that personality questionnaires reveal only your *perception* of yourself, which, as you are probably thinking, isn't necessarily the same thing as the way other people see you. However, the tests are very sophisticated, and in most cases (as I have found out myself recently) frighteningly accurate.

Will I be asked very personal questions?

No. Personality questionnaires are not puzzles or quizzes of the magazine variety; they never ask you about your favourite foods or your love life. The personality questionnaires used in recruitment simply assess aspects of your personality and character as they relate to the working environment, or a specific job.

What sort of questions will I be asked?

To give you a flavour of what to expect I have included two different practice personality questionnaires for you to try. As with all the other tests in this book (with the exception of the Combination Test) they are genuine practice tests from the biggest test publisher in the world, SHL Group plc.

As mentioned above, the only difference between these tests and the real thing is that real, live personality questionnaires have a lot more questions.

Test 30 Rating Statements

In this test you are asked to rate yourself on a number of different phrases or statements. After reading each statement mark your answer according to the following rules:

Fill in circle 1   If you strongly disagree with the statement
Fill in circle 2   If you disagree with the statement
Fill in circle 3   If you are unsure
Fill in circle 4   If you agree with the statement
Fill in circle 5   If you strongly agree with the statement

The first statement has already been completed for you. The person has agreed that 'I enjoy meeting new people' is an accurate description of him/herself.

Now try questions 2 to 6 for yourself by completely filling in the circle that is most true for you.

		Strongly disagree	Disagree	Unsure	Agree	Strongly agree
1	I enjoy meeting new people	①	②	③	●	⑤
2	I like helping people	①	②	③	④	⑤
3	I sometimes make mistakes	①	②	③	④	⑤
4	I don't mind taking risks	①	②	③	④	⑤
5	I'm easily disappointed	①	②	③	④	⑤
6	I enjoy repairing things	①	②	③	④	⑤

Test 31 Making Choices

This personality questionnaire has a different format. You are given a block of 4 statements: A, B, C and D. You must choose the statement which you think is most true or typical of you in your everyday behaviour, and you must **also** choose the statement which is least true or typical of you.

Indicate your choices by filling in the appropriate circle in the row marked 'M' (for most) and in the next row 'L' (for least).

The first question has been completed as an example of what to do. The person has chosen, 'Enjoys organising people' as most true or typical, and 'Seeks variety' as being least true or typical. Now try questions 2, 3 and 4 yourself.

I am the sort of person who...

1   A   Has a wide circle of friends

   B   Enjoys organising people

   C   Relaxes easily

   D   Seeks variety

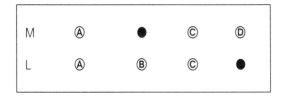

2   A   Helps people with their problems

   B   Develops new approaches

   C   Has lots of energy

   D   Enjoys social activities

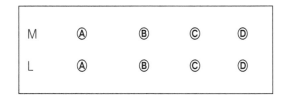

3   A   Has lots of new ideas

   B   Feels calm

   C   Likes to understand things

   D   Is easy to get on with

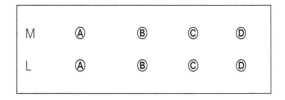

4   A   Enjoys organising events

   B   Sometimes gets angry

   C   Is talkative

   D   Resolves conflicts at work

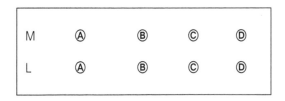

I'm finding it hard to decide which statement is **least** *like me – what should I do?*

I agree, it is difficult. In the past, when you took a personality test, there would always be several answer choices which stood out a mile as being the wrong ones. But not any more.

Here are some other examples of statements taken from 21st century personality questionnaires:

♦ Changes tasks willingly and grasps new ideas quickly.
♦ Communicates equally well with customers and colleagues.
♦ Pursues tasks energetically.
♦ Shares all relevant and useful information with the team.

You can see the problem. Which of these statements should you choose as being the *least* like you? They all describe qualities you'd imagine any employer would find highly desirable.

This test, and others like it are extremely clever because they are impossible to fudge. There are no obvious right or wrong answers. And the fact that there are no blindingly obvious 'least like you' answers, forces you to think hard about yourself and be honest.

And that's exactly what organisations who use these tests want – honesty.

Is it possible to cheat?

Modern personality questionnaires have sophisticated built-in mechanisms which can spot any deliberate lying or inconsistency only too easily. If you try to second guess the examiners by picking the answers you think they're looking for, your questionnaire is likely to be regarded as invalid, and your application rejected. Your only choice is to answer the questions as truthfully and honestly as you can.

The tests also have a huge number of questions, for example, as mentioned above, the *OPQ 32* has 230 items. The sheer size of the questionnaire makes it even more difficult to lie consistently – it might be possible at the beginning, but by the 100th question it'll be difficult to remember your own name, let alone which qualities you're pretending to possess!

Even if you manage to bluff or lie your way through the personality questionnaire, you'll still be found out. Interviewers like to talk about the results of the test, and then they often ask whether you agree with the results or not.

For example, if you've attempted to give the impression that you have, say, leadership ability, what are you going to say when your interviewer asks you to describe your leadership experience, or a time when you put your leadership ability to good use?

Besides, personality questionnaires are also about fitting the right people into the right jobs. By answering honestly, you're more likely to land a job that you enjoy and can do well.

However, there is nothing to stop you doing some research on the company in question to find out what qualities they look for in candidates. Many big firms are quite open about the personality traits they're after. Chapter Three covers how to research your chosen company to get hold of this information.

Having said that, even if you know what they want, it's in your own interest to be honest. For online personality questionnaires, that also means taking the test yourself!

Interest inventories and motivational questionnaires

In this chapter I have covered competency and personality questionnaires, however you could also be asked to complete an **interest inventory**, which is a questionnaire in which you are asked to decide how much you like carrying out various types of activities at work.

You could also come across something called a **motivation questionnaire** which looks at the energy with which you approach your work, and the different conditions which increase or decrease your motivation. I still maintain (as I did in my first book on psychometrics) that as far as motivation is concerned, your employer has a lot to answer for!

Personality Questionnaires – How To Improve Your Performance

With every other type of psychometric test I have been able to give you some suggestions as to how to improve your performance. However, with personality questionnaires, there are no tricks of the trade or useful exercises you can do. As I have already said, the most important thing to do is to **be yourself.** Remember:

◆ Personality and competency questionnaires do not have right or wrong answers. You don't have to worry about passing or failing – just concentrate on being honest, truthful and accurate.

◆ Make sure you answer all the questions. There may seem like a lot of them, but it is necessary to complete the whole test.

◆ Personality questionnaires do not have time limits, but try to work your way through reasonably quickly. This is particularly useful when being asked to decide which 'qualities' are most or least like you. Here, your intuitive answer is usually the most accurate – if you sit and think too hard you'll find the questions much more difficult.

◆ Some questions may seem completely irrelevant. Don't worry about this. Just answer as truthfully as you can and move on. The same goes for questions you don't fully understand. Do your best and don't leave any of the answers blank.

◆ Many questions ask you about the way you typically behave in a work situation. If you have no formal work experience, think about how you behave in similar situation at university or college or in other areas of your life.

◆ As mentioned above, many big firms actually list the personality traits they look for in graduate recruits on their web sites. Treat this information as a useful guide but don't try to second-guess the examiner – always be honest.

After taking a personality questionnaire, you should be offered the chance to discuss the results (and if the offer is not forthcoming, ask). Use the opportunity to find out as much about yourself as you can. Even if you are not offered that particular job, a better understanding of your strengths and limitations is always useful.

CHAPTER FIFTEEN

Management Tests

The tests in this chapter are not psychometric tests in the true sense of the word. However, I am including them because most employers view them as part and parcel of the same thing and use them widely when employing graduates.

Where will I encounter a 'management' test?

Generally you will be asked to take this type of test when you are invited by a potential employer to come along to their offices, or alternatively, to attend an **assessment centre**.

In other words, you will not encounter these tests until you are well into the recruitment process and have already passed through your target organisation's initial screening process. Therefore it is most unlikely you will be asked to take one of these tests online.

Note: Chapter 5 covers assessment centre visits and how to survive one. This chapter includes the tests and exercises themselves.

How do management tests differ from other psychometric tests?

The main difference is that these tests are more hands-on. Instead of filling in, or clicking, multiple-choice boxes, you physically usually write down your answers in the space provided on the test paper. And whereas with a multiple choice question you always have the opportunity to guess if you're completely stuck, answers to management tests usually require pretty hard thinking and also a certain amount of know-how.

For what sort of job would I be expected to take a management test?

The tests in this chapter are all used to assess graduates for management and junior management roles, especially those requiring analytical and problem-solving skills, across the whole spectrum of different industries around the globe.

What do management tests actually measure?

Whether you know how to manage. What sort of management style you have. How creative you are. How well you evaluate information. How logically you make decisions. How good you are at generating ideas and problem-solving strategies. How well you work under pressure...

Like traditional multiple-choice psychometric tests they also provide employers with a good indication as to a) whether a candidate has the right skills or aptitude for the job, and b) whether or not they will be successful in the job itself.

Who devises management tests?

They are written by the same test publishers who produce the traditional type of psychometric test, such as SHL Group plc. They are *not* devised by the company to which you are applying. However, many management tests are customised according to the individual company's requirements, so a management test taken at company A is very unlikely to be identical to a management test taken at company B.

Even if you do come across the same test being used by different organisations, the answers they are looking for may not be the same – everything depends upon the ethos, culture, management style, company goals and so on, of the organisation in question.

To get a clearer picture of what they are looking for you will need to do some research – see Chapter Three for information on how to do this.

Do management tests have right and wrong answers?

Some of them do, some of them don't. See the individual tests for clarification.

In a live test, will I get feedback on my performance?

Feedback on your performance in management tests is normally available – you will have to ask the test administrator at the assessment centre for details.

In this chapter there are six different management tests for you to try. There are three *Brainstorm* tests, one *Fastrack* test and two *Scenarios* questions – all very well known and extremely popular management tests used by a huge number of organisations to select graduate recruits.

I have also described a number of other management-type exercises that you will no doubt come up against when you attend an assessment centre or progress through a large organisation's recruitment process. These include:

- ◆ role plays
- ◆ group discussions
- ◆ in-tray exercises
- ◆ presentations
- ◆ interviews.

At the end of the chapter there is section entitled **Management Tests – How To Improve Your Performance** in which I explain ways you can improve your management skills without taking a management or business degree, and yes, it is possible!

Information on how to tackle the questions themselves are included before and after each particular type of test.

Please remember, however, that all of us have strengths and weaknesses, and everyone will have some difficulty with some of the tests in this book.

The Brainstorm Tests

These are very popular and widely used 'paper and pencil' graduate tests. They are designed to assess how productive an individual can be when coming up with ideas. In other words, your breadth of thinking. Brainstorms are used to assess graduates for management and junior management roles, especially those requiring analytical and problem-solving skills.

They consist of a number of work situations, or problems. What you have to do is read each work situation or problem, and then try to generate as many alternative options to the problem as you can in **four** minutes.

Sometimes the question will ask you for solutions to the problem. At other times it will ask you for explanations of factors that need to be investigated further. This will always be stated clearly in the question.

Four minutes per question is not very long (it's a deliberate ploy to put you under pressure) so work quickly and try not to dwell too long on each answer.

How are answers assessed?

There are no right or wrong answers as such, provided they are meaningful and relevant. Any organisation who presents you with this type of test will assess you on three things: the number of answers you give, the variety of answers, and the originality of the answers that you produce.

To sum it up, you are being assessed on your breadth and depth of solutions that are relevant. If you can explain your solutions in more detail, then go for it, but don't waste the time on just two or three answers.

What if some of my answers are completely impractical?

Brainstorming requires the generation of as many unusual or creative ideas as possible from lots of different angles. So don't worry too much about the practicality of your ideas – just try to think up as many as possible. You'd be surprised how many seemingly impractical ideas can be worked up, refined and made practical later.

How many Brainstorm problems would I have to tackle at an assessment centre?

Probably between six to eight.

As there are no right or wrong answers, how can I judge my performance?

Read the Self-Review guidelines, after the end of Test 34 Brainstorm 3. After you have completed the Self-Review, you might like to ask a friend or relative to have a go, and then compare the two sets of answers. This may generate other possibilities that you haven't thought of.

Also, as you work your way through the tests you'll notice how your creative ideas begin to flow. It's a little bit like turning on a tap; the water trickles out to begin with, then flows faster and faster. The first time I tried Brainstorm I only managed 3 decent ideas. The second time I thought up 26. So try the tests and watch your creativity catch fire.

Instructions for Tests 32, 33 and 34

Instructions: Each Brainstorm test contains a different problem. In each case, depending on the wording of the question, you are required either to give as many explanations as to why the problem has occurred, or to suggest as many solutions as you can to the problem that has been set.

If this is not your book, then I suggest you write your answers on a separate piece of paper. When recording your answers, keep your writing legible. In a live test the test administrator can't award you any marks unless he or she can read what you've written!

Time guideline: Allow yourself 4 minutes for each test. This will give you a realistic feel for the time you will be given when you take the real thing.

Test 32 Brainstorm 1

You are the Marketing Manager of an organisation that is planning to open up a new health club and gym on a greenfield site on the outskirts of a town.

List as many ways as you can to publicise this new venture to attract new members to get the gym off to a good start:

1 _____

2 _____

3 _____

4 _____

5 _____

6 _____

7 _____

8 _____

9 _____

10 _____

11 _____

12 _____

13 _____

14 _____

15 _____

16 _____

17 _____

18 _____

19 _____

20 _____

Test 33 Brainstorm 2

Here is another Brainstorm for you to try. The instructions and time guideline are printed before Test 32.

You are the Managing Director of a company with a small IT helpdesk that is responsible for supporting the IT needs of the rest of the organisation. You are having significant difficulties retaining people in this role. They tend to leave after a couple of months just as they start to become productive.

List as many possible reasons as you can for the high staff turnover in this function:

1 _____

2 _____

3 _____

4 _____

5 _____

6 _____

7 _____

8 _____

9 _____

10 _____

11 _____

12 _____

13 _____

14 _____

15 _____

16 _____

17 _____

18 _____

19 _____

20 _____

Test 34 Brainstorm 3

Here is another Brainstorm for you to try which I think is rather fun. The instructions and time guideline are printed before Test 32.

You arrive at work expecting to give a detailed presentation to your boss and other senior managers only to discover the paperwork, which you have been preparing for the last three weeks, is securely locked inside your desk. What do you do?

1 _____
2 _____
3 _____
4 _____
5 _____
6 _____
7 _____
8 _____
9 _____
10 _____
11 _____
12 _____
13 _____
14 _____
15 _____
16 _____
17 _____
18 _____
19 _____
20 _____

Self-Review for the Brainstorm Tests

Brainstorming requires people to generate as many unusual or creative ideas as possible that can be refined and made practical later. Work your way through the following self-review questions and use these to help you to focus on what you must do when you take the test for real:

◆ How did you find the time pressure? Four minutes is not very long so you need to be quick, and not dwell too long on each answer. Try to generate as many different answers as you can in the time.

◆ How legible are your answers? Although you need to work quickly, your answers will be read by an assessor. Feel free to write in short note format, but make sure it is comprehensible to someone else.

◆ How creative were you? One of the secrets of brainstorming is to generate as many ideas and from as many different angles as you can. Do not worry too much about the practicality of them – this happens later.

◆ Did you read the question carefully? One example asked you for suggestions to the problem and the other asked you for explanations of it. You need to ensure that your answers were appropriate in each case.

◆ Once you have completed the Self-Review you might like to ask a friend, colleague or relative to have a go, and then compare your answers. This may generate other possibilities that you had not contemplated.

Now you have taken the Brainstorm tests and worked through the Self-Review, you should feel much more comfortable with this type of test should you encounter it during your job search. You know what to expect, you've had some valuable practice, so you should feel a lot more confident as a result.

Test 35 Fastrack

Fastrack is a card-based test measuring problem solving and analysis aptitude. In other words, it tests how you think.

In order to successfully complete this test you will have to:

◆ Understand the problem you are presented with.
◆ Identify information relating to the problem.
◆ Identify patterns within this information.
◆ Generate the correct strategy to solve the problem.
◆ Apply this strategy and decide on the answers to the problem in question.

Like all the tests in this chapter, Fastrack is used to assess graduates for management and junior management roles, especially those requiring analytical and problem-solving skills. The only difference between this test and the real thing is that at an assessment centre you'll probably be given five different problems to tackle instead of one.

Test 35 does not require the use of a calculator, however please note some Fastrack tests do require one.

Instructions: On the opposite page you will see 10 boxes (at the assessment centre these will be made of card). The first box marked Situation P contains instructions, the rest contain information. The information in two of the boxes is incomplete.

It is your job to look at the boxes with complete information, work out the underlying rules and patterns, then complete the missing information in the spaces provided on the two answer sheets. If you cannot reach a decision, mark your best choice but avoid wild guessing.

Note: It may be helpful to photocopy the page, so that you can then cut out the 10 boxes and spread them out on a desk in front of you, re-ordering them as you wish (due to copyright restrictions please only photocopy this book for your own use).

Once you have made a decision as to the answers to the questions, check them by comparing them to the correct answers on page 152.

Time guideline: Once you're happy that you know exactly what you're expected to do, allow yourself 7 minutes to work on the actual problem.

Test 35 Answer Sheet

Tick the relevant box to indicate whether the Priority Code should be High or Low:

CARD Priority Code

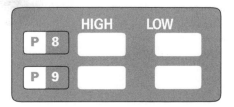

Indicate the Machine Time in hours:

CARD Machine Time

P SITUATION P *INSTRUCTION CARD*

PAA Foods plc manufacturers 'own-brand' cleaning products for supermarkets.
Cards P1–P9 represent outstanding orders from clients.
Based on the completed cards, establish the priority codes and machine times where they are missing.
Mark your answers in the Answer Sheet section.

P 1 MONDAY 24 HourStores

Order Quantity	32,000 units
Previous Orders	200,000 units
Process Code	P106
Priority Code	**LOW**
Machine Time	**8 hrs**

P 2 MONDAY Cambridge Provisions

Order Quantity	30,000 units
Previous Orders	75,000 units
Process Code	Y654
Priority Code	**LOW**
Machine Time	10 hrs

P 3 TUESDAY Brook Ltd

Order Quantity	12,000 units
Previous Orders	450,000 units
Process Code	Y654
Priority Code	**HIGH**
Machine Time	4 hrs

P 4 TUESDAY HYY Stores

Order Quantity	12,000 units
Previous Orders	350,000 units
Process Code	Y654
Priority Code	**LOW**
Machine Time	4 hrs

P 5 MONDAY Chaundry & Sons Ltd

Order Quantity	16,000 units
Previous Orders	450,000 units
Process Code	P106
Priority Code	**HIGH**
Machine Time	4 hrs

P 6 TUESDAY Kent and Co

Order Quantity	32,000 units
Previous Orders	400,000 units
Process Code	J765
Priority Code	**HIGH**
Machine Time	4 hrs

P 7 WEDNESDAY Cook & Watson Ltd

Order Quantity	32,000 units
Previous Orders	400,000 units
Process Code	P106
Priority Code	**HIGH**
Machine Time	8 hrs

P 8 THURSDAY Saver Stores

Order Quantity	48,000 units
Previous Orders	250,000 units
Process Code	P106
Priority Code	**?**
Machine Time	**?**

P 9 THURSDAY Poundright

Order Quantity	6,000 units
Previous Orders	200,000 units
Process Code	Y654
Priority Code	**?**
Machine Time	**?**

Answers are given on the next page.

Answers to Test 35

The answers include an explanation for how they were reached, which you might find very useful for understanding the thought process that goes into the making of the Fastrack test.

CARD Priority Code

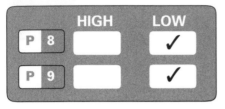

In order to establish the missing Priority Codes it would have been useful to order the cards into two columns in front of you, one column for High Priority Codes and the other for Low Priority Codes.

When the Previous Orders are 400,000 units and above the Priority Code is High.

For Previous Orders of less than 400,000 the Priority Code is Low.

CARD Machine Time

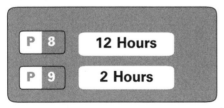

In order to establish the missing Machine Times it would have been useful to re-order the cards into two columns, one for Process Code Y654 and the other for Process Code P106 (card P6, Process Code J765, is irrelevant).

For Process Code P106 you can see that for an order quantity of 32,000 units the machine time is 8 hours and for 16,000 units the machine time is 4 hours.

The rule here is that for Process Code P106 it takes 1 hour for every 4,000 units.

For Process Code Y654 you can see that for an order quantity of 30,000 units the machine time is 10 hours and for 12,000 units the machine time is 4 hours.

The rule here is that for Process Code Y654 it takes 1 hour for every 3,000 units.

The Scenarios Tests

Scenarios is a 'paper and pencil' test designed to assess an individual's understanding of everyday management situations, as well as the effectiveness of the individual's responses to these situations. In other words, your managerial judgement.

Companies who use it want to know whether you have the basic knowledge and know-how to make an effective and successful manager.

Knowing how to manage, however, is not exactly the same thing as *actually* managing – for this companies use personality questionnaires such as the *OPQ* and also assess your performance during management exercises (see **Other Management Tests** below).

Like all the tests in this chapter, Scenarios is used to assess graduates for management and junior management roles, especially those requiring analytical and problem-solving skills.

Time guideline: There is no time limit for the completion of the two Scenario example questions, however allowing yourself around three minutes for each one will encourage you to work quickly and prevent you pondering too long on any one item. But don't set the clock until you've read the instructions (below) and familiarised yourself with the rating scale.

Instructions: First of all have a good look at the rating scale printed below.

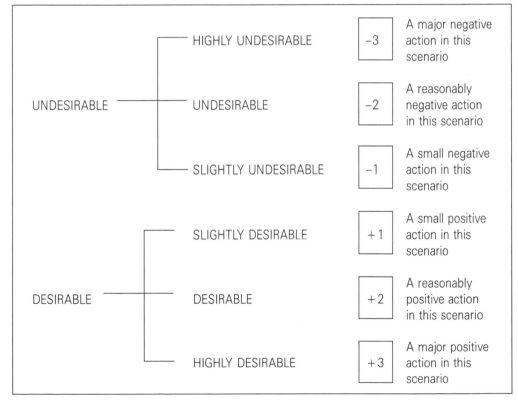

Now read the text of the first Scenario problem and the five different response options listed underneath. For each response option, decide whether you think it is an undesirable or desirable course of action. Once you have made up your mind about that, decide exactly *how* undesirable or desirable the option is, as per the rating scale shown above.

For example, if you think the response option is an extremely good idea, give it the highest rating of +3. If you think it's a terrible idea, give it a −3. You can, of course, choose any of the ratings in-between those two extremes.

Note your answers down on a piece of paper, then have a go at the second Scenarios test. Then read my explanation, which will give you a pretty good idea if your answers are, from a business and management point of view, in the right ball park or not.

Please note there is no answer sheet to fill in. Because of the complexity of this test, I felt it would be better to explain how to go about tackling it. But in the live Scenarios test, you will be given the usual psychometric test-type answer sheet complete with lots of little circles to fill in.

Test 36 Scenario 1

You have just been promoted to run a department which was reputedly well managed and highly effective under your predecessor. She has subsequently been promoted to a new post within the organisation in another part of the country.

During your initial few months you would:

1   Personally conduct an immediate and critical review of all existing departmental policies and practices.

2   Inform your staff that you will be making no major changes to the department for at least 6 months.

3   Ask your staff for ideas on how to make further improvements to the department.

4   Write an article on your department's aims and objectives in a local business journal.

5   Get involved in several interdepartmental project teams as a means of getting to know your management peers.

Test 36 A Howard & M Choi, 1998, revised 2001

Test 37 Scenario 2

You supervise a team of 6 people and are responsible for overseeing their work on a daily basis. Your immediate manager is generally happy with your performance, but has voiced concerns over your recent scheduling of overtime. Specifically she wonders why overtime is invariably necessary on a Friday afternoon. You have explained that workload is very heavy with just six staff and there is an urgent need to ensure work is completed before the weekend – otherwise customer delays will result. Your manager is not convinced and has asked you only to schedule paid overtime after direct consultation with her.

However, the following Friday a fault has developed with your customer systems which, although rectified four hours later, has caused considerable mayhem to your team's schedule. If the backlog is not cleared, you know there will be irate customers next week. Several of your team offer to stay on to address the backlog but if you allow this, overtime pay will be necessary. However, your manager and others at a comparable level have gone to an off-site meeting and cannot be contacted.

You would:

1   Schedule the paid overtime and deal with the consequences later.

2   Respect your manager's decision and send your team home with a view to tackling the situation on Monday morning.

3   Explain to the staff that this is a team problem and therefore everyone needs to remain behind and work unpaid overtime.

4   Send you team home but stay on yourself for a few hours to salvage what you can from the situation.

5   Have a brief report of your reasons for scheduling paid overtime on your manager's desk before her return on Monday.

Test 37 A Howard & M Choi, 1998, revised 2001

Answers to the Scenarios tests

As mentioned above, there are no right or wrong answers provided for this test. However, now read my explanation below, including the notes headed **Four More Things**. If your answers are broadly similar to mine, you'll know you're on the right track. If your answers are completely different then hopefully my explanation will get you back on track.

Scenarios 1

1   This response is probably not a good idea. It could be argued that this response is an obvious choice for a new manager getting to know his department. However, I think the word 'critical' implies that you might be seen to be raring to make changes just for the sake of it. This could alienate staff and even be perceived as quite threatening. Therefore I'd give this a low rating, probably a –3.

2   Informing staff you will not be making any changes is another bad idea. A lot can happen in six months, and it would be a foolish manager who promised otherwise. I'd give this a –2 or a –3.

3   Asking staff for suggestions on how to improve things is a good idea. I would have preferred the question to have been worded slightly differently, because *only* asking for improvements could be seen as a criticism. However, as you have no choice but to work with the given wording, I'd still award this a +2.

4   As a new manager, writing an article in the local paper would surely be totally inappropriate at this early stage. Therefore I'd give this response a low rating, probably a –2 or a –3.

5   Getting involved would be a good way to learn what makes your department tick. If you got to know your management peers as a result, that would also be a bonus. Therefore I'd give this response a high rating, probably a +3.

Scenarios 2

1   The way I see it, you have *got* to get the work done for the sake of the company. Therefore this response must be awarded a high score, say +2 or +3, even though there may be hell to pay on Monday. Personally I'd prefer the response option to read,

'Schedule the paid overtime and buy your manager a mobile phone,' but it doesn't.

2   My immediate reaction to this was that surely the right answer depends on the culture and ethos of the company in question. Then I realised that managers are paid to make tricky decisions, and clearly waiting until Monday would be disastrous. Therefore I'd give this response the lowest rating possible, –3.

3   This could create a lot of bad will. Why should anyone be forced to work late on a Friday evening for nothing? Good managers are considerate and reasonable, therefore I would give this a very low rating, perhaps a –3.

4   Considering what needs to be done is at least a six-man job, how much could you realistically expect to achieve by yourself? Not much. However, I suppose it would be better than doing nothing, so I'd give this response a +1, but no higher.

5   This is perhaps the best idea of all. You salvage the situation, keep your staff happy *and* explain your actions, hopefully pre-empting any criticism.

Four more things you should know about Scenarios

◆   Firstly, in the live test, you will be given a psychometric test-type answer sheet complete with lots of little circles to fill in.

◆   Next, when taking the Scenarios test, resist the temptation to give alternative answers. I have to admit that when confronted with Scenarios for the first time I felt like scribbling. 'It's impossible to answer this question,' but that would not have helped. You *must* follow the instructions, and rate each response option as per the rating scale.

◆   The same goes for explaining your reasons, or changing the wording of the response options. *Only* consider and rate the choices given, and *only* fill in the answer sheet according to the instructions.

◆   Don't worry if you find some of the response options difficult to rate. Pick something (never miss out a question) and move on. In a live Scenarios test you will have, wait for it... up to 100 responses to rate! This is a good thing. It's your performance over the entire test which counts, not any one particular answer.

◆ Finally, a tip from SHL themselves: try to be decisive. A good manager will either reject an idea, or go for it, not sit on the fence. I'm not advising you to avoid the middling scores of –1 and +1 completely, I'm merely suggesting you avoid picking them 100% of the time.

Other management tests

Here is a brief description of other tests and exercises you may be expected to carry out during an assessment centre visit (or as you progress along a large organisation's recruitment process) especially if you are aiming for any sort of management or trainee management position.

Role plays and group discussions

These are exercises for groups of candidates, involving a discussion in which each individual takes on a specific role. Here's an example:

> *You are the Board of Directors of XYZ company and you are planning to move premises to either ABC or DEF location – discuss the impact of this decision.*

Each candidate is expected to negotiate from their own perspective, for example, one of you could be instructed to take on the role of Finance Director, another could be Marketing Director, another could be HR director, and so on.

These role plays can also be one-on-one, for example:

> *You are a manager and you have a meeting with a member of your team who is not performing. What do you do?*

Throughout the discussion or role play you will be observed by experienced managers from the recruiting company who will decide whether to offer you a job based on your performance (as well as your performance in psychometric tests, interviews and possibly other exercises, such as a presentation).

Note: Rather than sitting around a table, you could be asked to carry out a physical task together with some of the other candidates. Be prepared for this, especially if you are aiming for a position involving technical ability.

By putting you in this situation, the organisation can clearly see how well you get on with other people, whether you consider other people's views, how you work in a team, how you cope under pressure, what position you assume in the group, whether you're willing to compromise, if you can conjure up relevant and creative ideas, whether you get involved or sit on the sidelines ... the list is endless.

The trick is to try to ignore the selectors sitting on the sidelines scribbling silently into their notebooks, and try to enjoy yourself. It *is* a very pressurised situation, but remember all the other candidates will be feeling the same way as you. Whatever you do, always be considerate towards the other candidates. *Never* rubbish another person's opinion, however ridiculous it is, and don't get into an argument.

In-tray exercises

This is another very popular management exercise. Here's an example question:

> *You are a trainee marketing manager for our company. It is 3 p.m., and in two hours time you will be leaving for a week's holiday. However you still have 15 items in your 'in-tray' which need tackling. Put the 15 items in priority order, and then explain your reasons in writing.*

In-tray exercises test your ability to prioritise, evaluate, make good business decisions and work under pressure – all necessary management skills.

The trick is to decide which tasks are the most important to the business and put those ones at the top of your list. Whatever you do don't pick items simply because they're dead easy, or quick, or sound like fun. Evaluate each item carefully, think about the consequences if they get left for a week, take note of who wants you to attend to them (ie the managing director), and whether they are date sensitive or not.

Asking you to explain your reasons in writing is intended to prevent candidates picking the order of items at random without giving the problem any thought.

Presentations

Here you are expected to talk to an audience on a given subject for several minutes, either with or without advanced warning. The audience will include people from the recruiting organisation and quite possibly other candidates.

Popular subjects are those relevant to the recruiting organisation's business and also items (such as hobbies) you've included on your CV. Possibly the hardest thing to deal with is being asked to choose your own subject, when the most articulate person's mind can go completely blank. Be warned – canny candidates often carry prepared notes in their briefcase, just in case. Why not be one of them?

Alternatively, you may be asked to interpret and analyse certain information and present a case to support your decision.

If you've been given advance warning, prepare thoroughly and always try out your presentation on your friends or family beforehand.

The trick is to keep your presentation simple but interesting. Talk to the audience, not the flipchart (if you use one), try not to send everyone to sleep and always, always be professional in your manner. That means no swearing, rude jokes, racist comments or silly walks. And smile.

As with group role plays and exercises, giving a presentation will put you under considerable pressure – and I'm afraid that's the intention. Remember that all the other candidates will be feeling just as scared as you, so always give them your support and encouragement.

Interviews

These need no introduction, however, at an assessment centre be prepared to be interviewed either by a panel of people, or in a group along with other candidates. If you can answer the following questions confidently you'll do well:

- What do you know about this company?
- Why do you want to work for this company?
- Why are you interested in this job?
- What would you contribute to this company?
- How do you think you'll make the transition from university to employment?
- What have you gained from your university years?
- How do you get on with your classmates/tutors?
- What's been your greatest non-academic achievement?
- What are your strengths and weaknesses?
- How well do you work in a team?
- What are your career objectives?
- Where do you see yourself in five years' time?

In a *structured* interview you may be asked about examples of situations when you have demonstrated particular skills, or how you would tackle specific problems. There's more about this in Chapter 14 under competency questionnaires.

Management Tests – How To Improve Your Performance

What if you are not taking a management or business degree – how can you possibly improve your management skills? Here are some ideas to help you not only tackle management tests, but your career in general:

- Make the most of your time at university. If you intend to go into management, get some management experience now. How? By joining different clubs and societies and playing an active role in them. Don't just go along – offer to help, find out what needs doing and get on with it.

- Alternatively, organise your own club or society from scratch. Setting it up, attracting members, organising venues, times and dates, motivating people to get involved and stay involved, dealing with finance – these are all immensely valuable management skills which will not only help you shine whenever you come up against a management test but can be used to greatly enhance your CV as well.

To improve general performance in management tests

◆ Take an interest in current business news, read the business press and business journals. Remember to research the company – see Chapter 3 for how to do this.

◆ Talk to people you know who work in a business environment, or run their own businesses, about the kind of management problems they encounter and how they deal with them.

◆ Expect to be set questions asking how you would deal with specific staff problems. This because:
(a) in a management role you will be expected to do just that, and
(b) staff problems, as opposed to say, customer problems, are usually the trickiest ones to deal with.

◆ When tackling written problems, always read the questions extremely carefully to make sure you know exactly what you have to do.

◆ During group exercises and role plays, try not to be distracted or fazed by the observers. They are just doing their job, not trying to intimidate you. Like you, they'll also be longing for a cup of tea or even more likely, a big stiff drink!

CHAPTER SIXTEEN

What else do psychometric tests test?

As we've seen in Part Two, there are many different types of psychometric test. Some measure your ability to work or reason in a certain way, some claim to analyse aspects of your personality and character.

But there are three things that **all** psychometric tests measure.

◆ Firstly, your ability to turn up on time, settle down, concentrate and work hard for a reasonable amount of time.

◆ Secondly, your ability (or lack of it) to follow instructions and work neatly – absolutely essential if you want to score any points at all on any kind of psychometric test.

◆ And lastly, of course, your ability to understand precisely what you are being asked to do.

These are qualities **every** organisation looks for in its staff, including its graduate recruits. They want your timekeeping to be reliable. They want you to be able to settle down and work quickly and effectively and not mess about. They want you to respect the organisation's culture and follow laid-down procedures, not make up your own rules as you go along. They want you to get on with your job and not waste time pretending to be ill, gossiping or playing computer games.

Asking a bit much, I suppose, but some people are unable (or unwilling) to do any of these things.

Your references may not be entirely honest. Your CV may exaggerate your achievements. You may be able to impress whole armies of interviewers with a show of confidence, charm, friendliness and even sex-appeal.

But with a psychometric test, you are on your own. You can see why employers like them so much.

PART THREE
Psychometric Tests in Context

CHAPTER SEVENTEEN

Pyschometric Tests in Context

However much psychometric tests are lauded as the fail-safe, scientific method of selecting the best candidates, and however widespread the use of them grows, I really don't think employers will ever come to rely on them completely. The good news is that psychometric tests will always be just a part of the recruitment process, a powerful tool but not the only one.

You'll never be hired purely on the strength of a test – once you've got through the initial stages of a selection process (which shouldn't be a problem now you have this book) you will always have your chance to impress at an interview.

And for those of you who are still quaking at the knees, let me reiterate:

1   In a psychometric test you do not have to score 100% to pass. Many organisations set the 'pass' level as low as 50%. The whole point of the test is to eliminate candidates who are totally hopeless, so they can concentrate on the rest of you.

2   Most ability-type tests are not designed to be finished in the time set. Giving you more questions than you can reasonably cope with in the allotted time is a deliberate ploy. Taking a psychometric test is meant to be stressful.

3   You can improve your test performance considerably by familiarisation and practice – the reason you bought this book!

CHAPTER EIGHTEEN

Avoiding psychometric tests altogether

What if, despite hours of practice and bank accounts full of therapy, the thought of taking a psychometric test still makes you feel like hiding under the bed? Is it possible to avoid taking psychometric tests altogether?

Well, given that a growing number of companies subject potential employees to some sort of testing in addition to the traditional face-to-face interview, it may not be possible to do this, especially if you are applying to large companies.

However, there are a number of possibilities that do spring to mind. The most obvious one is to apply for a job with an SME.

Working for an SME

Before you decide that the only organisations worth working for are BIG ones, consider the alternative. A smaller company (an SME) may have just as much, or even more to offer.

Note: The definition of an SME varies according to who you ask! To give you a rough guide, an SME is usually an organisation which employs up to 50 people, and/or a turnover up to £20 million. So 'small' can mean anything from absolutely tiny, to really quite large, well-established and vastly successful companies.

Here are just some of the advantages of working for an SME:

✓ More responsibility, earlier on.
✓ The chance to work directly with the directors or owners of the business.
✓ Greater variety of work.
✓ The opportunity to learn every aspect of how a business works.
✓ Reasonable starting salaries (SMEs know they have to compete with the big boys).

✓   A real chance to be a big fish in a small pond.

It's also much easier to land a job with an SME than a large company because their recruitment processes are usually simpler. After you've submitted your CV and letter, huge numbers of SMEs still rely on a couple of interviews to pick their people. Of course, I can't absolutely guarantee that. An ability test to determine your suitability for a specific job (for example, having to analyse a set of figures when applying for a statistics job) is still a very real possibility. But with an SME you are certainly less likely to be given a psychometric test, and very unlikely to be required to attend an assessment centre, give a presentation, or have your Lego building capabilities scrutinised.

Just why this should be so isn't clear. Perhaps it's because most SMEs (and certainly the smaller ones) do not possess full-time personnel departments. Perhaps it's because they simply don't have the time and resources to drag the recruitment process out for longer than absolutely necessary.

Perhaps it's because directors of small firms, who often interview applicants themselves, are confident about their abilities to pick the right people without recourse to additional methods of selection. I call it the '*I can recognise the right candidate as soon as he/she walks in,*' syndrome. Whether it works or not, thousands of company directors still suffer from it; a situation psychometric test publishers are working very hard to change.

So before they succeed, I would definitely recommend you consider working for a SME.

Working for yourself

Becoming self-employed could be an area you haven't even thought about. It would certainly appeal if you are the sort of person who:

◆   likes the autonomy of making his or her own decisions
◆   is happy to work alone
◆   is extremely determined
◆   is prepared to forgo the security of a guaranteed salary.

Successful entrepreneurs also have to be very organised and hard working. They are frequently charismatic and creative risk-takers with leadership ability. They are usually confident, always intelligent, and they need to be able to get on well with others.

And because fashions, industries and economies are constantly changing, successful entrepreneurs have to be prepared to face a never-ending stream of challenges and problems. However, if you have a product or service that people want, and you are able to offer a professional and reliable service, there's every chance that in time, you could become very successful indeed.

Of course, working for yourself has its downside too. You will have to market your product or service in order to find customers – which can be very difficult. You may not have a boss telling you what to do, but you'll still have masters: fickle customers, unreliable suppliers, and whoever you've borrowed money from looking over your shoulder. Furthermore, it may take a long time to build up a regular clientele, which means your income stays lower for longer than your employed friends.

But one thing is certain: if you work for yourself, no one will ever expect you to take a psychometric test!

Starting your own business – list of resources

For help and advice on becoming self-employed, try:

- Business Link www.businesslink.org
- Inland Revenue www.inlandrevenue.gov.uk/startingup
- Small Business Service www.sbs.gov.uk
- The DTI www.dti.gov.uk
- Federation of Small Businesses www.fsb.org.uk
- The Prince's Trust Business Club www.princes-trust.org
- www.bt.com/sme or www.bt.com/getstarted
- Your relevant trade organisation.
- PLUS: talk to people you know who are already running their own businesses. Ask them about their experiences and the problems they've faced. They'll soon bring you down to earth if your expectations are unrealistic.

CHAPTER NINETEEN

Resources

Help and information on the Internet

www.prospects.ac.uk
Extensive site for graduates, with loads of career and job-hunting advice, plus jobs.

www.careersa-z.co.uk
Information on hundreds of different careers.

www.hobsons.co.uk
A top site for career advice, information on employers, graduate vacancies, placement work and term-time jobs.

www.milkround.com
Find out about graduate recruiters, vacancies, recruitment events, recruitment agencies plus news and advice.

www.shldirect.com
Easy to navigate site includes careers guidance, help with the assessment process and free practice ability tests and personality questionnaires.

http://work.guardian.co.uk
Great inter-active job site has free practice psychometric tests plus lots of work related news.

www.ase-solutions.co.uk
Example abstract, verbal and numerical questions, plus practice questions for their best known psychometric tests GMA, 16PF5, FGA (First Graduate Assessment), GAT2 and MOST.

www.jobserve.com

Good recruitment site for a multitude of different industries, especially IT.

www.gradrecruit.co.uk

Good site for recruitment jobs in a wide range of industries.

www.hotrecruit.co.uk

Thousands of part-time and temporary jobs, including lots of extraordinary and simply crazy jobs. You can check out the jobs without having to register, which makes a change.

www.brain.com

Lots of free IQ, acuity and memory tests plus lots of articles on brain topics.

www.advisorteam.com

Take the free Keirsey Temperament Sorter and discover whether you are an Artisan, Guardian, Rational or Idealist. Also IQ tests and free newsletter.

www.testingroom.com

US site offering free tests on topics such as personality, career values, career interest inventories and career competencies.

www.majon.com/iq.html

Another interesting US site includes IQ test selection area, with information on the main US postgraduate college entrance exams (all high-level psychometric tests) including GRE, LSAT, GMAT, MCAT and SAT.

www.9types.com

Entertaining personality questionnaire site.

www.opp.co.uk

Articles on psychometric testing (mainly aimed at employers but interesting nevertheless).

www.infomaticsonline.co.uk

Career and job-hunting advice, useful tips for taking psychometric tests and links to online tests, plus jobs.

www.computercontractor.co.uk
Computer industry jobs, help with CVs and interviews, plus information on psychometric tests with plenty of example questions.

Alternatively just do a search for 'graduate recruitment' and you'll be spoilt for choice.

University web sites

University web sites often have lots of useful career information and job-hunting help, especially for graduates. Many include tips on taking psychometric tests.
Some good ones are:

www.keele.ac.uk
www.graduatecareersonline.com (Manchester University)
www.careers.lon.ac.uk (London University)
http://www.shef.ac.uk/careers/students/applying/ (Sheffield University)

For help and advice on becoming self-employed, see the resource listing at the end of Chapter 18.

To save yourself the bother of typing all these web addresses yourself, just surf to my web site, www.shavick.com click on *careers*, and then on *career link page* and you'll find all the links ready to use.

Further Reading

CVs for High Flyers, Rachel Bishop-Firth (How To Books, 2004)

Graduate Career Directory (Hobsons, published yearly). Career and job-hunting advice plus hundreds of employer profiles.

Handling Tough Job Interviews, Julie-Ann Amos (How To Books, 2004)

Landing Your First Job, Andrea Shavick (Kogan Page).

Pass Psychometric Tests, Andrea Shavick (How To Books, 2003).

Pass That Interview, Judith Johnstone (How To Books, 2005)

Successful Interviews Every Time, Dr Rob Yeung (How To Books, 2004)

Turn Your Degree Into a Career, Dr Michael Collins and Benjamin Scott (How To Books, 2003)

Write a Great CV, Paul McGee (How To Books, 2001)

Index